Now Listen

I'm going to count to 519 and this time I'm serious!

Now listen

I'm going to count to 519 and this time I'm serious!

A troubleshooting guide for parents

Sarah Reid

REED

For Caleb, Samuel and Kristin.
My own wonderful guinea pigs.

Published by Reed Books, a division of Reed Publishing (NZ) Ltd,
39 Rawene Rd, Birkenhead, Auckland. Associated companies,
branches and representatives throughout the world.

www.reed.co.nz

This book is copyright. Except for the purpose of fair reviewing,
no part of this publication may be reproduced or transmitted in
any form or by any means, electronic or mechanical, including
photocopying, recording, or any information storage and retrieval
system, without permission in writing from the publisher.
Infringers of copyright render themselves liable to prosecution.

ISBN 0 7900 0736 3

© 2000 Sarah Reid

The author asserts her moral rights in the work.

Text designed by Graeme Leather
Cover and illustrations by Kevin Wildmen

First published 2000

Printed in New Zealand

Contents

Introduction	7
How to make your child feel loved	9
Respect for parents	11
Bath and shower time	13
Bedtime	15
Bedwetting	18
Birthdays	20
Building self-esteem	23
Bullying and teasing	25
The Bunny Principle	27
Car travel	28
Changing nappies	31
Charts	33
Chores	37
Cleanliness	39
Clothes	41
Competitiveness	42
Co-operation	44
Dealing with anger	47
Dealing with grief	51
Discipline	54
Disobedience	57
Disrespectful talk	59
Eating	60

Fighting over toys	63
Games	65
High chair high jinks	68
Hitting and biting	69
Holidays	71
'I'm bored'	73
Learning to talk	75
Leaving your child with someone else	77
Making friends	82
Messy play	85
Nagging	87
New baby	89
Pocket money	91
Potty training	93
Shyness	94
Spoiling children	95
Sulking	97
Swearing	98
Television and computers	99
Telling tales	101
Trips	102
Waking too early in the morning	104
Waking up in the night	105
What teachers wish new entrants knew	107
Whining or baby talk	109
Crafty ideas for preschoolers	111
Party games for preschoolers	125
Some fun ideas for school-aged children	127
Further reading	139

Introduction

My sewing machine came with a little book telling me how to use it. At the back of the book is a page called 'Troubleshooting', which offers advice like, 'If the light doesn't go on, try plugging it in' and 'If it makes a horrible noise, put oil in all the little holes.'

Wouldn't it be great if kids came with advice like that? 'If the engine keeps running after you've put it away, unplug it' or 'If fluid leaks out of the bottom in a supermarket, return it to the manufacturer.'

This book, sadly, is not a complete troubleshooting guide to parenting. I guarantee that not everything here will work with your child. But I also guarantee that many things in this book will.

So, before you pack the children up and return them to the manufacturer, have a glance through these pages.

The chapters are arranged in alphabetical order, except for the first two: 'How to make your child feel loved' and 'Respect for parents'. I feel that these two are the most important, and all our strategies for dealing with children come back to our love for them, and their love and respect for us.

Remember: love is spelt T.I.M.E.

Most kids will turn out okay no matter what we do, so let's determine to have fun and enjoy parenting along the way. These days are so short!

May God strengthen you in your awesome job as a parent.

How to make your child feel loved

~

We all know that we love our kids, but sometimes that love gets lost between us and them, like a heat-seeking missile with a flat battery. Somehow we haven't communicated our love in a way that has reached them. Here's a checklist to try:

♡ Make eye contact when you are talking with them.

♡ Squat down on the floor — come to their level when they are telling you something.

♡ Touch them. Hugs, rubbing their back or head, rough and tumble on the floor, sitting them on your knee, or a gentle punch. These all speak love.

♡ Give them time. Little and often is best. Allow them to interrupt you (at appropriate times) to tell you things or ask questions. Big chunks of time are beyond value too, when you shut out the world and give your full attention to this one child. It could be a walk together, teaching them a skill, involving them in your world, getting involved in their world, playing, making something or having a 'date' over a milkshake.

♡ Listen without interrupting. Smile, nod and raise your eyebrows.

♡ Give specific praise. 'I like the way you painted the clouds all swirly', and 'Thank you for putting your shoes away.'

- ♡ And general praise. 'I'm proud of you', 'I love you', 'I'm glad you're my kid.'

- ♡ Little gifts speak love to some children. Or a postcard when you are away, a note left on their bed and so on.

- ♡ Get involved in their interests. Instead of just dropping them off at ballet or rugby practice, stay and watch.

- ♡ Try to recognise your child's 'love language'. Is it:
  — touch?
  — doing things for them?
  — praise and encouragement?
  — giving gifts?
  — time alone together?

> You can have an interesting discussion asking the children to work out their own love language. (See *The Five Love Languages of Children* by Gary Chapman and Ross Campbell, and *How to Really Love Your Child* by Ross Campbell.)

Respect for parents

It is vital that our very young children learn to respect us as parents, for five main reasons:

1. The parent-child relationship is the first of a lifetime of relationships, and forms a model for all the others.
2. A lack of respect for parents will lead to a lack of respect for other authorities — teachers, bosses and the law.
3. Children who see their parents as unworthy of respect will turn into teens who have no time for their parents' values.
4. Without respect for the parents, family life can be chaotic.
5. Children need boundaries to feel secure. The parent who sets up and enforces clear boundaries gives a message: 'You are safe and the world is under control.' It is a scary thing to find yourself the smallest yet most powerful person in the house. Kids test the boundaries, not because they want to knock the fences down, but because they want to make sure the fences are still there!

Yeah, yeah, we know all that, but how do we get the little cherubs to respect us?

- ♥ By respecting them and treating them with dignity.
- ♥ By our showing respect to their other parent, and other adults.
- ♥ By ensuring that they feel loved and heard.
- ♥ By loving firmness. Parents need to win most of the battles, but always try to be fair. There's a big difference between respect and fear.

RESPECT FOR PARENTS

Here's the game plan for winning most of the battles.

1. Make sure he knows the rules. (Don't eat all the strawberries.)

2. Tell him the consequences of disobeying. (If you eat all the strawberries, you won't get any fruit tomorrow.) See the chapter on 'Discipline' for some ideas about consequences.

3. Now if he *deliberately*, *coldbloodedly*, *haughtily* chooses to disobey you, you discipline him in the agreed manner. It's that wilful disobedience that needs to be disciplined. Remember, though, at the same time we are showing respect for him, so we never belittle or criticise him, or discipline him in front of his peers.

For children under eighteen months, these three steps are shortened to:

1. A firm 'No!'

2. A consequence if she repeats the behaviour.

> Choose very carefully which battles to enter. Does it really matter if he dyes his hair? If she sleeps upside down in her bed? If he jumps in the puddles? If she steps out in front of that bus? Since you need to win most of the battles, consider carefully:
> - Can I win this one?
> - Is it worth a fight?

Also, try to say 'No' seldom, so that when you do say it, it is heard. 'Dad, can you play with me?' You want to say, 'No, I'm busy', but you could try 'Okay. After tea I will play with you for ten minutes' or 'What a good idea. Let's see if we have time when I've finished this.'

The word 'No' can shut a door of communication but a wait-and-see-I-like-your-suggestion sort of answer keeps it open.

Our children will be more likely to respect us if we are approachable, fair and fun, loving and respectful, and if they know that we mean what we say.

Bath and shower time

If she is reluctant to get in:

♡ explain that we need to keep clean to stay healthy and smell nice for other people; tell them about a time when you met someone who didn't wash — pooh!

♡ let her choose some plastic utensils from the kitchen to take into the bath

♡ take some ice cubes into the bath and watch them melt

♡ take some coloured water (half a teaspoon of food colouring in a plastic cup full of water); tip it in and watch it spread

♡ put a candle on the window sill and turn the light off

♡ eat fruit or raw vegies in the bath

♡ take soap into the paddling pool instead

♡ have a tape recorder in the bathroom

♡ have a bath with your child.

If it's still a problem, try the Bunny Principle (see page 27).

After that, you may need to talk to her at another non-threatening time, about any fears she may have — of drowning? of getting burnt? of being left alone?

If she still won't co-operate, you could try the Indonesian style of washing, a mandi. Stand her in the bath and gently tip a bowl of warm water over her, from the shoulders down. Soap all over, then another bowl of warm water. Or you could sit her in a small plastic basin of water in the bath and wash her in that.

If he is reluctant to get out:

♡ take the plug away!

Showers

♡ An adult-sized shower cap keeps the water off their faces.

♡ They could take a child's umbrella in for a few minutes to get started.

Hairwashing

Some children hate having their hair washed, or even getting their head wet. You could try these ideas:

- ♡ Have the baby in the shower with you from an early age, if she likes it. This ensures she is used to the feeling of water running over her face and it may not be an issue later on. Use a child-friendly, non eye-stinging shampoo.

- ♡ Use the lie-back method. Hold the child like you did the baby in the bath. Your arm goes right round the back of his head and your hand grips his upper arm on the far side. His head lies in the crook of your elbow or above it. Then you gently use a cloth to scoop water onto his hair.

- ♡ Children's hair doesn't actually get as greasy as adults', so providing her hair isn't too long or too thick, you could simply wipe her hair with a damp cloth to remove the honey and mud. You may get away with this for weeks before a shampoo job is necessary. If you find this idea too gross, try wiping with a soapy cloth, then a rinsing cloth.

Bedtime

Bedtime can be a nightmare for parents, especially when other parents talk about what a warm, cosy time it is for them. Here are a few tips to head us all in the warm, cosy direction.

♡ Establishing routines can help. The child knows what to expect of you, and what you expect of him.

♡ The pattern could go something like this:
  1 bath
  2 tea
  3 brush teeth and toilet
  4 horsey ride to the bedroom
  5 story
  6 song
  7 sleep.

♡ From tiny babies, get them into the habit of going to bed awake, so they expect to fall asleep in bed. This way they don't need you in order to get to sleep, and they don't get a fright when they fall asleep in your arms and wake up somewhere else.

♡ Some children want you to stay with them until they fall asleep. Don't do it! It's a trap!

♡ Instead promise to pop back after five minutes to see how they are. Make sure you do! Then praise them for staying quietly in bed. You may need to promise another return in ten minutes and so on.

BEDTIME

- ♡ You could sing a song as you leave the room, so your voice gradually fades away. This makes the parting less abrupt. Or sing a line each so the child is responding as you fade away.

- ♡ Let him look at books for five minutes. This settles him down and also encourages good reading habits.

- ♡ Have a non-leaky drink bottle beside the bed of older children so they don't need to bother you for water. Also a potty on a plastic sheet in the room might help.

- ♡ Door open and light on in the hallway might help some children, but young children generally aren't afraid of the dark unless we unwittingly suggest to them that they might like to be!

- ♡ Do something quiet and boring yourself for half an hour, so she doesn't feel she is missing out on anything. Turn the television off and read the paper or do the dishes.

BEDTIME

But if they don't settle, then what?

♡ If they keep crying it could be because they have learned that crying works. ('Last night I thcreamed and thcreamed and Mummy gave me water and hugth and let me thee *Clarke and Nanthy* for five minuteth. I wonder if *Clarke and Nanthy* ith on again tonight?')

♡ We may need to train ourselves not to reward their crying. Don't go in at all. Especially don't wait until she is really screaming before you go in, because then you are actually reinforcing screaming. Even a baby of a few months old can figure this one out. 'If I cry a wee bit, no one comes, but if I keep hollering they show up. I'll just keep hollering.'

♡ If you absolutely have to go in, wait for a slight lull in the battle cry, so you are rewarding the lull, not the crying.

If they get out of bed:

♡ silently take them back to bed. Don't talk! Even that is a reward. Imagine you are a robot. Now resume at step 7, not step 4 with horsey rides.

♡ see the chapter 'Waking up in the night'.

For more help see an excellent little book, *The Sleep Book*, by Kathy MacDonald.

Bedwetting

There are whole books on this subject, so the main advice from this one is: Don't worry about it. It seems that about 20 percent of four-year-olds wet their bed, more commonly boys, but most of these will be dry by the time they are seven. At that stage you could see a doctor or public health nurse to talk about alarms and so on. But in the meantime …

- ♡ Do whatever makes you, the washer of the sheets, least stressed. Is he okay about a nappy? Then go for it! Disposable undies? Fine! If he feels too grown up for these, you could try making your own system. Secure a disposable nappy inside some tight-fitting bike shorts, with pins, or more expensively, those sticky velcro dots. You could chop off the fold-over parts of the nappy to make it seem less nappy-ish.

- ♡ Lifting them in the night and taking them to the toilet may work for some, but for others it only teaches them to let fly while they are still half asleep.

- ♡ Rewarding her for being dry doesn't seem to help much either, but I reckon you should give yourself (in secret) a chocolate bar every time she's wet, because you had to do all the extra washing. You must have burned up 100 calories hanging out those sheets in the wind. (Eat it with your meal though — less fattening.)

- ♡ We all know we must never scold and show any sign of annoyance, but sometimes it's hard to be calm and positive at 2 a.m. on a frosty morning. Honestly, though, the child can't help the bedwetting.

BEDWETTING

♡ Restricting fluids before bedtime seems logical, but it doesn't seem to make any difference to kids learning bladder control while they are asleep.

♡ However some drinks like grapefruit juice and Coke (as well as tea, coffee and alcohol) encourage the body to pass fluid, so these could be avoided.

♡ You could try bladder-stretching exercises during the day. When he wants to unload, suggest that he wait two more minutes. The next day it might be four minutes and so on.

♡ Older children will have a fluid-catching arrangement under their sheet, like plastic, rubber or wool. If clean sheets and pyjamas are laid out in their room they could change the bed themselves and avoid embarrassment.

For further help see an excellent resource, *Bedwetting*, by Glen Stenhouse and Michael Watt.

Birthdays

Why is it that the birthday child throws a wobbly and cries? Here are some ideas to avoid this:

♡ Explain before the day that although this is her day, it's not a day to be selfish. We invite friends around so that we can share our happiness with them, not so they can give to us.

♡ Tell stories about kings and queens who used their birthday to give presents to poor people.

♡ Warn him that he may receive presents he doesn't like. Tell him what to do if that happens: 'Say thank you anyway, and come and tell me later.'

♡ If she grizzles about a present being 'dumb', you will take it away and give it to someone else. Children often say this about a toy that is too challenging for them. All the same they can learn to be patient, to wait until we have time to help them, and until they have a chance to grow with it.

♡ Let him be part of planning the day; that way he is involved as a host, a giver more than a taker. Together plan the food, the games, and pack the loot bags if you are having them.

♡ I let the children help in decorating the cake. Our birthday cake book is the most used book in the house by children, and the cakes are not hard.

♡ Although we love to give our children what they want, we must remember that they'll expect the same, or more, next year. So keep it simple.

BIRTHDAYS

Some ideas for parties

♡ Have a theme for the day, for example a colour, a letter, an animal, a television programme, or a sport. Costumes, games and food can centre around the theme.

♡ Have a picnic in an unusual place. In winter you could be in a culvert, under a bridge, or in a band rotunda. Take a tape recorder with you to set the scene and play games there if possible.

♡ Visit a friend with puppies or kittens.

♡ Send a metre of material with each invitation. Each child must make a costume for the party, or a nightie for the sleepover.

♡ Girls might enjoy a teenager coming to demonstrate how to put on make-up.

♡ A video and popcorn.

♡ A hike.

♡ A make-your-own-sundae. Put out ice cream, chocolate sauce, hundreds and thousands, nuts, bananas and so on.

BIRTHDAYS

- ♡ Go fruit picking.

- ♡ Go to the beach (winter or summer — see the chapter on 'Trips').

- ♡ Make your own water slide. Buy five or six metres of black polythene from a garden shop and hold the hose at the top. It works best on a slope, but on the flat sprinkle washing powder, or for sensitive skins, rub a cake of soap over the polythene.

- ♡ A river party; swimming; body boarding.

- ♡ See the chapters on 'Games' and 'Party games for preschoolers'.

Building self-esteem

Self-esteem is whether we feel good or bad about ourselves. We get it from the things we hear about ourselves, and the things that happen to us.

A child who is told, 'You're thick', eventually believes she's thick and behaves like a thick person. A child who is told, 'You'd better stay inside and not play rough games', eventually believes he is weak and behaves like a weak person.

The good news is that low self-esteem can be unlearned and high self-esteem can be learned.

Try some of these ideas in your family:

♡ The suggestions in the chapter 'How to Make Your Child Feel Loved'.

♡ Praise them for specific things they have done. Not just, 'Good boy', but, 'I like the way you put your coat away.'

♡ Don't add a 'but' to your praise. 'Wow! You tidied your room! Why can't you do that all the time?' or 'You were good at Mrs Smith's but you forgot to say thank you for the drink.' The 5:1 rule about praise tells us to give five words of encouragement to one word of criticism.

♡ Think of your praise as silver boxes, something precious for your child to take with him into the rough, tough world.

♡ Don't praise them for things they haven't done, or be sarcastic.

♡ At the dinner table, go round each person stating one thing that he or she is good at, or one thing you like about their personality, appearance, talents, hobbies, friends and so on.

BUILDING SELF-ESTEEM

- ♡ Write notes to your kids telling them what you like about them.

- ♡ Tell other people, in your child's hearing, how great your child is. I heard of a woman who introduced her children according to their talents: 'This is Simon — he's the musician in the family. This is Heather — she's the caring one — and Jo's the scientist.'

- ♡ Don't criticise your kids to other people, even when they can't hear. We may have to change our opinion of them before they can change their opinion of themselves.

- ♡ Accept praise on behalf of your kids. When you hear, 'They were good today', you can reply, 'Huh! They're never good at home!' or 'Oh, that's great. Thanks for having them.'

- ♡ Remind yourselves what you like about your children, and what they are good at.

- ♡ Set limits and rules and stick to them.

- ♡ Be specific about the behaviour you are disciplining them for. (Not 'You have been so naughty all day' but 'Because you glued the cat to the floor …')

- ♡ Celebrate their achievements. Have a special plate (it may be the old chipped one) that is only used when someone gets a certificate, learns to ride without trainer wheels, starts kindergarten and so on. Ring Grandma or a friend and let the child tell what they have done or learned. Display their artwork at home.

> Let's tell our kids:
> ✓ You can do it.
> ✓ I believe in you.
> ✓ I'm proud of you.
> ✓ I'm glad you're on my team.

Bullying and teasing

Kids can be cruel. Every child will be the victim of bullying at one time or another, and as parents we feel like rushing in and 'sorting it all out'.

But if we can teach our children to handle the situation themselves, then they have won the battle, not us. Just as it is better to give a man a fishing rod and teach him to fish, so it is better to give our children strategies rather than stepping in and flattening the first bully that comes along. Try these ideas:

♡ Actively listen to him telling you what is going on. Don't offer advice at this stage; just ask questions that clarify the picture. Questions like, 'What happened next?', 'How did you feel?', 'What could you do about that?'

♡ Now teach him to react calmly — not to cry or run away but:
— to say, 'Stop that, I don't like it'
— to walk away
— to find someone else to play with
— to say what they do want: 'That's my bike and I want it back.'

♡ Explain that bullies are often being bullied themselves and we can feel sorry for them. They are often cowards who feel small inside. They try to push other people down to make themselves feel bigger. But your child is already big on the inside. She is strong and good and no one can change that.

♡ Explain that bullies push the green button to make the red light come on. If the red light doesn't come on, eventually they will stop

BULLYING AND TEASING

pushing the green button. If you don't cry, run away or give him what he wants, he will soon get bored and give up.

- ♥ Talk to her about how she is reacting. Role-play the situation as she has been responding, then how she could respond.

- ♥ Use the Bunny Principle (see page 27). 'Bunny just smiled and walked away when Fluffy laughed at his new shorts, so Fluffy stopped laughing.'

- ♥ Give him some good responses to verbal criticism, not further put-downs that will give the bully more fuel for his fire. For example, not 'So what if I can't kick the ball, you can't sing.' Instead, 'I know I'm not very good at sport but I'm trying and I enjoy it' or 'Yes, I wear glasses now. They are a pain but they help me to see, so I'm glad of them.'

- ♥ In extreme cases it may be necessary to contact a teacher or the police, or to speak to the bully's parents.

The Bunny Principle

≈

A great way to help young children deal with all sorts of problems is to make up stories about a character who comes to grips with all the things with which they are grappling. Things like sharing toys, hitting other children, being left with a babysitter, visiting the dental nurse, anything at all that is an issue in the child's life.

I call it the Bunny Principle because our character was always Thump the Bunny. We had stories about Thump's friends coming over to play, but Thump wouldn't share his toys so they all went home again. Thump felt sad and left out. Or you could use the child's own teddies and act out situations, like a role-play.

These stories help children to identify their feelings and see how their actions affect other people.

Car travel

Here are some ideas to make travelling in the car more bearable.

♡ Pack a 'lunch box' for each child, containing all the food they will need for the day. This way they eat when they want to, and you can cater for individual tastes.

♡ Pack an 'entertainment box' for each child. A few nibbles, puzzle books, pencils, cards, small video games, comics, plastic animals, sunglasses, hat and all the trinkets they collect on the trip.

♡ For children who get car sick: don't give them things to do which will make them look down; try to keep eyes forward and up. Avoid dairy food such as milk, ice creams and so on. Savoury foods can help, like chips. Ginger is good for preventing car sickness — try ginger ale, gingernuts, preserved ginger, or ginger from a health food shop. Putting fingers out the window can help, as can sitting in the front, and fresh air.

♡ Plan to stop regularly, especially where there will be toilets and a playground. If possible, plan to do the long stretches when the darlings will be asleep.

♡ If you are travelling for several days, let each child be boss of the car for a day or half a day. The boss allocates seats, chooses games and tapes and suggests stops.

♡ A Walkman each, or one for the person whose taste in music differs from the majority.

CAR TRAVEL

Some car games

♡ Find things out the window that start with each letter of the alphabet. The first person might find an aeroplane, the second person a bike and so on. Go around in a circle.

♡ Again in a circle, each think of something starting with the letters. Topics could be boys' names, girls' names, body parts, food (vegetables, fruit), towns, countries.

♡ Guess the distance. The driver chooses a landmark ahead on the road — that haybarn, that hedge on the right. All the passengers close their eyes and each say 'Now' when they think the car has reached that landmark. Then they open their eyes, but keep quiet until everyone has said 'Now'.

♡ Car collection. Each person chooses a different colour. You score one point for every car of that colour which comes towards you.

♡ 'I'm thinking of a person ...' One person thinks of someone who everyone knows (maybe a relative, friend, rugby player, famous person). The others ask questions that can only be answered yes or no. Begin with questions like, 'Is this person alive?', 'Is it a girl?', 'Is he younger than me?'

♡ Serial story. Go around in a circle, each one contributing a paragraph or two to a story. Adults should start and make it crazy, to capture the kids' imagination. 'Once a three-legged guinea pig with a yellow sun hat, called Frizzy, fell out of a plane ...'

♡ Quiz. Mum or Dad is the quizmaster, asking questions of each child in turn, according to their age and knowledge. 'Who is Barbie's boyfriend?', 'Name the nine planets in the solar system.'

♡ You could award a small lolly or nut for a correct answer. A hint for the quizmaster: to keep your mind from going blank, work your way through topics, for example maths, television, vegetables, trees, space, rhyming words, spelling, geography, history, books, animals.

CAR TRAVEL

♥ Cricket. One person comes in to 'bat'. Points are scored from the number plates of oncoming cars. You get one point for every letter on the number plate, but B = bowled, C = caught, L = LBW. If traffic is sparse, use the numbers on the plate too. Each number is worth one, except 4 and 6, which are, predictably, worth four and six.

> By the way, look back over each of these games and notice their educational value!

Tiny tots in the car

For littlies who are too small to see out the window, my best piece of advice is tapes. First sell your car and buy one with a fade button on the stereo. This allows you to direct the music to the back (or front) seat. Try borrowing tapes from the library until you find the sort your child enjoys. Probably simple, repetitive songs will appeal the most. I know you can't stand to hear *Jingle Bells* for the fortieth time, but it's better than 'Waaaa' for the fortieth time! With the fade button you can listen quietly to the news in the front once she has nodded off.

Changing nappies

When littlies are turning into biggies and trying to wriggle away, smearing brown ooze as they go, you might like to try these ideas:

♡ Use a soft, warm surface to change him on. He might be slightly more inclined to stay if it's comfy.

♡ Have everything ready before you grab her: wet cloth, clean nappy and so on. Think of yourself as the pit stop in a stock car race.

♡ Give him something to play with.

♡ Have something unexpected pinned to your sweatshirt that will catch her eye and slow her down for ten seconds — a safe brooch, a ribbon or button on a safety pin, a rattle on a string, a balloon around your neck and so on. Little fiddly things pinned onto Mum's clothes are also good when breastfeeding older babies who get restless.

♡ Sing and jiggle around as you change him, to make changing a fun time together. Or tickle his face, neck and tummy with your hair and with kisses.

♡ If she cries, blow gently in her face. This will give you one second more to complete the task while she draws breath.

♡ If he still insists on trying to escape, it may be time to use a short, sharp smack. This needs to happen in a very structured way, as follows:

1 Our hero makes a bid for freedom by starting to roll over.

CHANGING NAPPIES

2 You say 'No!' very firmly.

3 You follow, one or two seconds later, with one smack on the bare bottom or thigh.

4 Usually hero cries while you complete the change, then give him a cuddle.

The 'No!' is very important. In time you will only need to say 'No!' and suddenly he thinks to himself, 'Hello. That word again. Last time she said that I got sore. I'll just lie still and see what happens.' Thus he learns to obey your command.

Charts

~

> Charts are a wonderful way to encourage appropriate behaviour and most children respond well to them, if they are regularly kept, but they don't work if the adult forgets to fill them in!

Sometimes we can feel that our kids should be above this reward-for-good-behaviour sort of system. They should just be good because it's the right thing to do. But hang on! How many of us would turn up for work on Monday morning if we weren't going to get paid on Friday afternoon? As adults we operate on a behaviour-reward system, so why shouldn't kids?

Charts for younger children (three to six years)

Rule lines of squares onto a piece of paper, about ten squares per horizontal line.

Each time he does something you approve of (obeys the first time he is asked, does something without being reminded, shares and so on), a tick, star or stamp goes on the chart. Stickers aren't necessary, and you need to feel free to be generous.

When a horizontal line is filled a reward is given. It might be a chocolate fish, 50 cents, an extra half-hour up at night, a turn on the computer and so on. Whatever it is, decide on it beforehand.

♡ Make sure the reward is available straight away, because if she has to wait to receive it, the reward loses impact.

♡ Be generous with your ticks. Give two or three at once if he tidies up without even being asked. Initially you will need to be giving out the reward every two or three days so he gets the message that this chart thing is cool. Once he is hooked, the lines can be longer and ticks given less liberally.

♡ As she learns to obey the first time you ask, soon you will be able to noisily find a pencil, walk over to the chart and with pencil poised say, 'Kate, would you put your pyjamas on, please?'

♡ Display the chart in a prominent place.

♡ Use a pencil for the ticks so you can rub them off in order to discipline inappropriate behaviour: 'If I have to ask you again, I will rub a tick off.'

Charts for older children (six to ten years)

When children have outgrown the simple chart, a more elaborate one is good. On the left-hand side list the things you want accomplished, and along the top list the days of the week.

Things to do	Mon	Tue	Wed	Thu	Fri	Sat	Sun
Get ready for school by 8.30	✓	✓	✓				
Feed the dog		✓	✓				
Get changed after school	✓	✓					
Music practice	✓						
Other		✓✓					

CHARTS

♡ The squares are ticked each day as the task is completed. You could say they only get a tick if they do it without being asked. Definitely only if they do it with a good attitude.

♡ The space 'Other' is for extra things you ask them to do, or for using their initiative to do things without being asked.

♡ Charts are different for different children and the things they are required to do.

♡ Parents need to be diligent to keep up with marking the charts, or the system quickly falls down.

♡ You choose how to reward the ticks. You could:
— at the end of the week award five cents for every tick that week and perhaps 20 cents for the ticks on 'Other'. This then becomes their pocket money.
— count the ticks in one week. If there are fewer than, say, 20 ticks, they get no pocket money that week; if more, then they receive their pre-arranged amount.
— count the stars at the end of every day. Five stars means he can watch television, have pudding, play on the computer and so on. Less than that — no reward at all.

Negative charts

Negative charts are not as good as positive ones where you reward good behaviour. But in some situations, for a brief period of time, they can work and be used to stamp out *one* specific behaviour, like hitting, swearing, grizzling and so on.

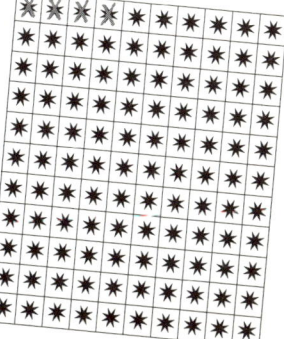

Make a chart, about ten squares across and eight lines or so down, and fill it in before you begin, with ticks, stamps or stars.

♡ Now you cross out one square, in pen, every time the behaviour occurs.

CHARTS

- Each line represents a week. At the end of the week award a lolly, five cents, or time on an activity for every square that isn't crossed out.

- In the first few weeks you won't be parting with many lollies, but towards the end of the chart you'll be dishing out a lot. One chart should do the trick. Have a break for a few weeks before you tackle another behaviour.

- Remember to give positive praise for the behaviour not occurring. This could be verbal, ticks on a positive chart, or hugs and praise: 'Well done, Nathan. You could have got upset when Bob ran over you with his bike, and I think you felt like swearing, but I'm proud of you because you didn't swear.'

- Another idea other than charts is to make a pile of five cent pieces at the start of the week. Say, 'You can have all this money on Friday, but each time you swear [hit, bite] I will take away one coin.'

Chores

Helping around the house is good training for kids. It takes some stress off the parents, it shows children the need to pull their own weight in the world and it contributes to good self-esteem.

- ♥ Even three-year-olds can have a job to do every day: set the table, feed the cat, clear the table, pull the curtains and so on.
- ♥ Encourage them to take pride in the job and to go the extra mile: put flowers on the table, make placemats, play dinner music for the cat ...
- ♥ Gradually increase the responsibility with age.
- ♥ As children come to realise that this is their own particular area of responsibility, a simple 'Good' or 'Thank you' should be sufficient reward. But while they are learning, you could put ticks on a chart or give pocket money for the task done each day (see 'Charts'). I tend to say, 'You have to do the work anyway, but if you do it with a good attitude you will get the tick on the chart.'
- ♥ We must make sure we are setting a good example and not insisting he picks up his things if we don't pick up ours!
- ♥ Don't reward every little thing. Kids need to learn to do things just because we all work together, not because there is a reward every time they shut a door.
- ♥ Work together.
- ♥ Set aside a specific time for chores, like Saturday afternoon, all hands on deck.

CHORES

- ♡ They might enjoy loud music while they work.

- ♡ If it's a major tidy-up, like leaving to go on holiday, or cleaning up the holiday house before you come home, make a list of jobs to be done. Dish out the first job to each person, then as they finish that they can choose their next one.

- ♡ When drying dishes, to keep it fair between slowies and speedies, I ask everyone to dry twelve things each. (Hint: keep the cutlery in the sink and dry it yourself afterwards.)

- ♡ Kids love to count things. Ask them to find five things in the lounge that are in the wrong place and put them in the right place. This is more achievable than 'Tidy the lounge.'

- ♡ To make dusting fun, hide five old coins, plastic animals and so on around the room. They should find all five if they dust properly.

- ♡ Explain that they do things for you, and you do things for them, like … (the list is endless).

- ♡ If you ever have a threatened mutiny on your hands ('I'm not taking the rubbish out any more!'), you could say, 'Oh, I see. So we're not doing things for each other any more.' Then a few hours later, or when the situation arises, you can say, 'I'm sorry, I can't take you to the birthday party [wash your rugby jersey, cook your tea] because we don't do things for each other any more.' I'd save this idea for the big one, not just your garden-variety grizzle.

Cleanliness

≈

From the age of four or so, children can begin to take responsibility for getting themselves ready in the morning.

♡ Make a list, using pictures, which you stick on the fridge. She follows it to check that she has done everything before she goes to kindergarten. Your list might be shorter than this.

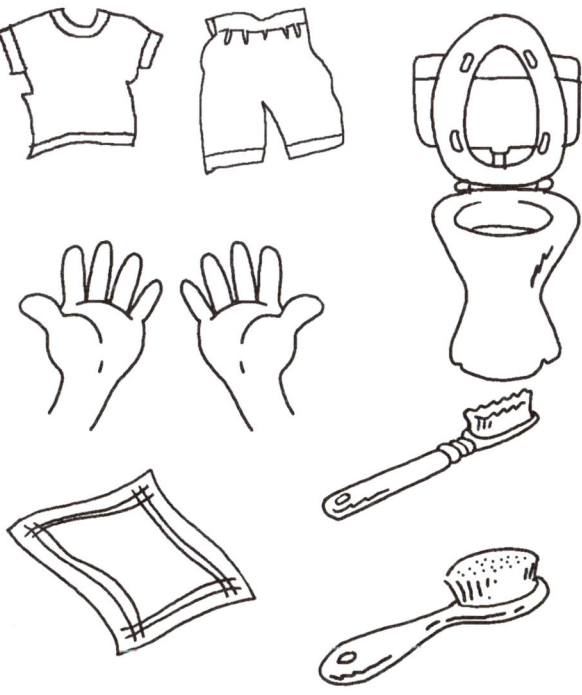

CLEANLINESS

♡ You could put a tick on a chart when she completes these things, without you having to nag, perhaps before the big hand of the clock gets to the bottom.

♡ Even older children need a reminder of all that's involved in a morning routine. Now the list will be in words, and maybe the fridge isn't a good place to hang it.

♡ Some kids are reluctant to have their finger and toe nails cut. Try tiny nail clippers or scissors, or let him file them himself.

♡ Brushing teeth can be a battle too. After you've tried all the yummy new toothpastes:
— show him your ugly black fillings
— explain how food sits on our teeth and turns to plaque. Plaque wears holes in our teeth and makes them sore. Then the nice dental nurse feels sad and has to put the black fillings in.
 — avoid negative and frightening talk about dental visits and fillings. You may live to regret it when you have to take him there!
 — you could use the Bunny Principle, creating a story about a character who didn't wash or brush his teeth. The others found he smelt bad and no one wanted to sit beside him …
 — an object lesson: use a stick of white chalk and poke at it with a pencil, to form marks and holes. 'This is what plaque does to our teeth if we don't brush them.'

Clothes

To encourage children to dress themselves:

♡ Start with the easy things — socks, jandals, some shoes, then undies, shorts and pants. Encourage any attempt to dress themselves. Give them time and try not to get impatient. ('Hurry up, please hurry up, oh do hurry up. Oh look, I'll just do it!')

♡ Say, 'I've got to go and make my bed. When I come back I wonder if you will have those pants on. Bet you won't.'

♡ Bring your clothes into her room and have a race, or do one thing each if she needs help.

If he is reluctant about wearing certain clothes:

♡ We need to look at our own attitude to clothes — hand-me-downs, labels and fashion. What message are we giving our kids?

♡ Try to distract him while dressing, by singing, telling a story or planning the day.

♡ Hide raisins in the pockets which he can look for when he's dressed.

♡ Use a Bunny Principle story to talk about the need for warmth and jackets to avoid getting sick.

♡ Make collage pictures. Draw two people, then cut out material and stick the things we might wear in summer on one person, and on the other the warmer things for winter. Talk about what could happen to the lightly dressed one if he went out like this in the winter. You could add snow, rain and sunshine to your pictures.

Competitiveness

Some children can't bear to lose. They throw a wobbly when they see themselves falling behind and hurl the Snakes and Ladders board across the room. No one in your family has this problem, of course, but someone you know could try these:

♡ Encourage games where you can't see who's winning until the end. Yahtzee is good.

♡ Short games like noughts and crosses. A loss isn't such a big deal because the game is over so quickly.

♡ Adapt the rules of games so people help each other, for example Scrabble and other word games.

♡ Eliminate the nasty rules, like sending people home in Ludo.

♡ Play games where losing is funny, like Spill the Beans, Jenga, and toothpick stack (see the chapter on 'Games').

♡ Do 'together' activities, which don't involve competing, such as puzzles, crafts, cutting and gluing.

♡ Do physical activities — walking, swimming, carpentry, climbing trees and cycling.

♡ Occasionally play the fiercer games, like snakes and ladders. Before you begin, talk about how you will feel if you don't win and what you could do.

COMPETITIVENESS

- As adults we must model good losing, and not taking a game too seriously. We could make a hilarious show of being a poor loser and help the child laugh at the situation.

- Let him win sometimes, but not all the time. He needs to be prepared for playing snakes and ladders in the real world!

Co-operation

'Nicholas, would you mow the lawn, please?'
'Certainly, Father, it would be my pleasure.'

Hey! Why are you gagging? Aren't your kids like this? Well, mine aren't either, but there is this wonderful thing called co-operation, which means he does what we want him to do, not out of fear or blind obedience, but because he wants to.

Why would he want to do that? Basically because:
— he knows we love and respect him
— he loves and respects us
— he wants to please us.

So ... how do we arrive at this heavenly state?

♡ Start with one behaviour at a time.

♡ Describe to yourself what it is you want her to do. (Get ready for bed the first time I ask.)

♡ Ask yourself whether you may have been rewarding her for not co-operating. Perhaps you expect to ask seven times, so her dawdling is rewarded by more time up.

♡ Now explain that there's going to be some tightening up: 'I know I've been slack in what I expect of you, but now I want you to go to bed the first time I ask.'

♡ When the time comes, leave what you are doing, go right up to her, establish eye contact, and ask in a pleasant soft voice what you want

CO-OPERATION

her to do: 'Raelene, go and get your pyjamas on and brush your teeth, please.' (Be specific rather than 'Go and get ready for bed.')

- ♡ If she does go straight away, then give heaps of praise, maybe an extra story and so on.

- ♡ If she doesn't, ask again, then take her. No praise. You may want to follow up with a consequence that you have already warned her about (see the chapter on 'Discipline').

Sounds easy? It's not. Not at first anyway, but it gets easier as kids learn what to expect and they learn to enjoy the positive attention (praise, hugs, thanks) that they get for co-operating.

Often as not, it's us parents who need to be trained, more than the children. We must teach ourselves:

- ✓ not to reward non co-operation with our attention, but to give attention to the obedience. Catch him doing it right and praise him.

CO-OPERATION

- ✓ to expect him to co-operate
- ✓ to ask firmly and pleasantly
- ✓ to follow through with our request, with praise for co-operation, and with another request and a consequence for non co-operation.

We will soon get into a flow and can use a system of do-this-and-you'll-get-that: 'Eat all your dinner and you can have pudding'; 'Get dressed and then you can go out to play'; 'Help me with the dishes, then you can watch television.'

If he is in the middle of doing something, a warning is a good idea, otherwise we can come across as an irritation; for example, 'In one minute I'm going to ask you to …' or 'Have one more turn each then …'

Young children can be diverted when they are considering not co-operating. When they are about to think, 'Will I do what she asked or not?', we jump in with another question to think about: 'Do you want to take Bunny or Green Ted to bed tonight?', 'Would you like a horsey ride or a piggy back to the bedroom?'

See *Good Behaviour*, by Fred Seymour, for more help on this.

Dealing with anger

~

It's not wrong to feel angry. Anger is an emotion, a feeling, and it's a healthy one. It can motivate us to help someone who is being treated unfairly, or to make good changes.

But it's what we do with our anger that counts. Violence and abuse are behaviours, they are not anger itself, and they are wrong. They have been learned and they need to be unlearned.

Children learn everything they know by one of three ways:

- ▲ by imitating (I saw this on television; my teacher showed me)
- ▲ by instruction (Mum told me what to do)
- ▲ by accident (I just tried this and it worked).

Violence is the same. Maybe he's seen it; maybe he hit someone one day and they ran away. Cool! As it was learned, so it can be unlearned.

We need to teach children that *it's okay to feel angry but don't hurt people, things or yourself.*

Teach them the words that go with the way they are feeling: 'You look really cross about that'; 'You sound angry'; 'That put you in a bad mood, didn't it?'

Play games to help with this.

♡ Make a face. She has to guess how you are feeling, for example angry, frightened, hot, sad, happy, tired …

♡ Reverse this and she makes the faces.

DEALING WITH ANGER

♡ Draw faces showing emotions. Cut them out and tell a story about what happened to a character and how she felt.

♡ Make puppets by drawing faces on wooden spoons. Make up a play to show what happened and how they felt.

We need to help children to see that they feel angry because something has happened to make them feel hurt, afraid or powerless.

Talk to your children about where in their body they feel the anger. Is it a tight feeling in their tummy? A hot feeling on their neck, ears or face? Is it in their chest? If they can feel anger starting, they can get ready to deal with it in a good way. Let them use colours to draw how they feel.

Help them to see anger like a flame. You can put more fuel on to make it bigger (talk about what sorts of things put more fuel on your fire); that's no good. You could pretend it's not there and try to sit on it or swallow it. Yow! You could let it die down. You could put the fire out.

DEALING WITH ANGER

First, let's look at things that people do to you: put-downs; name-calling; laughing at you; hurting you. Now let's look at the things that you might do, which could put fuel on your anger fire: hurting them back; shouting; slamming doors. None of this helps, does it? They just put more fuel on the fire and make us angrier.

So, we'll look at swallowing the flame, and see if that helps.

What do some people do to swallow their anger? (They go red in the face, say nothing, their eyes bulge, their mouth goes tight.) This can hurt them. Maybe not straight away, but later on, and it can even make people sick. It's called bottling up your anger. It doesn't help.

An object lesson: put a piece of wet bread in a jar. Leave it for a week, then talk about what has happened to it. Bottled up anger is like this mouldy bread; it doesn't get better if you leave it, but it gets worse. We need to get it out. Tip the jar upside down and talk about the need to let the anger out. The only way to let anger out is to talk about it, to use 'I' statements: 'I feel … when … I would like …', for example 'I feel cross when Darryl teases me. I would like him to say nothing.'

Now we could talk about ways to let the flame die down. Ask the child what, for them, makes the anger die down: going for a walk or a run? talking to the dog? watching the goldfish? reading a book? drawing a picture? writing a letter? having a story read to you? having something to eat?

Although the flame has died down, and that is good for the moment, it is still there, and it could roar back to life as soon as someone puts some more fuel on it. The fire of anger doesn't go out until we express it in words. The anger goes away when we talk about how we feel, using 'I' statements, and when we are listened to.

As adults, we may need to identify some of the three feelings — hurt, fear and powerlessness — in our own lives, to see why we get angry. What has happened to us? Is there still a flame simmering away inside somewhere that flares up unexpectedly? We may need outside help from a pastor, friend or counsellor.

Children learn more from watching what we do than by listening to what we say. So it is really important that they see us handling our anger — anger with the children and anger with other adults — in the right way.

Children who have an ongoing problem with anger, or quietness, may be victims of abuse and may need further help.

So ... great! She is able to tell you how she's feeling: 'I feeled weally pross when you took down my tent. I don't care if it wains an' I get washed out to sea.' Our job is to listen. Don't interrupt, don't justify yourself; just listen, nod and keep eye contact. You could say, 'Anything else?' Now praise her for expressing her anger so well: 'Thank you, Jenny, for telling me how you feel about the tent. Now I can see what made you angry and I can understand how you were feeling. Let's have a drink of milk and we'll decide what to do about it.' She may be happy to be heard and you may be able to leave it there. Or it could be appropriate to reach a compromise: 'Well, sweetheart, you can't sleep in the tent, but we can have a picnic lunch on a rug in the kitchen and pretend we are camping. [Diversion:] You go and choose which of your teddies to invite to the picnic.'

Remember: *It's okay to feel angry but don't hurt people, things or yourself.*

For more help on this, see *A Volcano in My Tummy*, by Éliane Whitehouse and Warwick Pudney.

Dealing with grief

Children experience grief over a great variety of things — a friend shifts away, a favourite toy breaks, a pet dies, parents separate, or a loved one dies. What may seem small to us can be devastating to a child because of the intensity of a child's feelings.

In many cases the grief will not last long and we as parents can show understanding and sympathy. But some children have to cope with a huge grief, like a death or separation, and we can help them to understand the stages of grief that they may be going through.

- Explain that it is normal to feel the way they do, and that it won't last for ever.

Denial

- It may feel like a dream, as though it hasn't really happened, or he may want to pretend it hasn't happened. This could be a way of protecting his heart until it is ready to face the truth. In cases of separation most children hope their parents will get back together, but few do. The arrival of another partner is a new crisis of grief, as it forces the realisation that there is no hope for a reconciliation.

Anger

- The child may feel angry at people, at God, at the doctors or at whoever was looking after them at the time. This, too, is very normal. It's okay to feel angry, but we need to be very careful how we act angry (see 'Dealing with anger' above).

To cope with grief anger:
— talk to someone about how you feel
— go to a lonely place and shout
— talk to a pet or a soft toy
— punch a pillow or scream into a pillow
— use up some energy by running, swimming, biking
— draw pictures to show how you feel
— write words to show how you feel, maybe a letter.

Overwhelming sadness

♡ Help her to understand that many other people feel as though their world has ended, and they will never stop crying. Crying does help; it lets some of the sadness out, and so does talking.

Guilt

♡ Children can feel that they are somehow responsible for a separation, or a death. We need to help them understand that it's not their fault. Some days they can feel quite normal; they get on with their day and forget to be sad. Then they can feel guilty about that. Tell them it's good to carry on, and the person they miss would want them to have more and more 'normal' days.

She may feel guilty about things she has said or done, and helpless that there is no way to put them right. Help her to talk about her feelings. Explain that no one is perfect all the time and that the person would have understood she was hurt and angry at the time. She could write a letter, telling all the things she wishes she had said or done differently.

Numbness

♡ A feeling of feelinglessness, like a dream or a fuzzy focus on television. This, too, is what other people go through and they do come out of it.

Fear

♡ Some children feel afraid of more disasters, of dying themselves, of being alone or of facing people. Again, help them talk about their fears; don't suggest they are 'silly', but together find practical ways to avoid scary situations.

Relief

♡ In some cases, for various reasons, there can be a sense of relief that this person has gone. Children don't need to feel badly about this. It's normal.

See *Everybody Hurts Sometimes: a book about grief for children and teenagers,* by Lois Tonkin.

Discipline

So he's decided to defy you, has he? You've identified that 'wilful disobedience'. Now what do you do?

Traditionally it seems there are four different ways to introduce a negative consequence, a bad buzz, a cold prickly. Some forms of discipline work better for some behaviours we are trying to discourage, or for some children. We have to choose the discipline that works for us, and our child, in each situation.

1. **A smack.** Perhaps one quick rap on the back of the hand.

    Advantage: It's over quickly. She knows she has been disciplined (and hopefully forgiven) and can get on with her life.

    Disadvantage: Some adults take this too far and it becomes abuse. A good rule of thumb is: If you are feeling angry at the time, then don't use this one.

2. **Time out.** Removing him to a certain chair or room (preferably not his bedroom where there are lots of toys) for a period of time, perhaps one minute or until he has calmed down. Some people suggest a minute for each year of his age. So a three-year-old stays in time out for three minutes.

    Advantage: He has a chance to cool down. It's good for social misbehaviour, like hitting. He misses out on the fun and togetherness that is going on.

    Disadvantage: Some kids get madder when isolated. It can be difficult to force a child to go to time out, but generally you can propel them from behind with your hands under their armpits.

DISCIPLINE

3. **Removing a privilege.** Missing out on pudding, no television for a week, no story tonight, no Cubs this week … Only for older children who understand; under two-and-a-half to three they need an immediate form of discipline.

   Advantage: You choose the thing that matters to her, thereby giving weight to the discipline.

   Disadvantage: The discipline can hang over the child all day, or for several days. Some children get more frustrated. Negative charts are, in effect, the removal of a privilege (see 'Charts').

4. **Chores.** 'If you two don't stop fighting I'm going to give you each a broom. <u>You</u> can sweep the garage, and <u>you</u> can get all the cobwebs off the house.'

   Advantage: He lets off steam, helps me, and is in 'time out', all a once. He knows I am boss.

   Disadvantage: If he is really steamed up, he might refuse to do the chore. Make sure you can win before you start. This one is more for the 'I've had enough of this behaviour' situation. It pulls the reins back in, then you start on a programme to shape behaviour. You could put 'black marks' on a chart. When they get five, they miss out on pudding or have to do the dishes.

> **Most of this advice is for children over three. Toddlers can usually be distracted when they are doing, or about to do, something wrong.**

- Give her something else to play with.

- Rush to the window and say, 'Well, well, would you look at that!'

- Have something interesting ready to show her for such a time as this.

- Start playing with a toy yourself.

- Look as if you are hiding something. His curiosity will drive him to forget whatever it was he was doing.

DISCIPLINE

♡ Praise her for doing it right, or meaning to do it right even if it ended up a mess, rather than waiting to tell her off for doing it wrong.

♡ Arrange your house so he can fiddle with everything he can reach and not risk harm to himself or to your precious stuff. Children need to have access to their own home.

> **Remember: be easy on yourself. We all make mistakes and treat our kids unfairly. We all regret it. Don't be afraid to say 'Sorry' to her. This also helps her to say 'Sorry' to someone else later.**

Disobedience

~

Sometimes our darlings keep doing something that they know we can't stand, despite our discipline, our charts and our attempts to bring co-operation. We may need to step back and ask, Why is she doing it? It could be for one of these reasons:

- **To get attention**. Did you know that rats prefer cages with random electric shocks to cages with nothing to do? That's not to say that your kids are rats. Not at all. Just that intelligent creatures, like children, and rats, prefer to be yelled at and punished than ignored. We need to ask ourselves if we've been spending enough quality and quantity time with our kids, filling up their emotional tank so they don't need to seek attention. If they are seeking attention, give it to them!

  Catch him being good and praise him. Don't be sarcastic: 'Gosh, I've just looked out the window and the tyres on the car haven't been slashed. Thanks for that.' And don't add barbed wire to the bunch of flowers: 'You were so nice to Mrs Blossom. Why can't you speak to me like that?'

- **For revenge**. To get back at someone for what they see as an injustice. You might need to get to the root of the problem and talk about 'What happened?', 'How did you feel?', 'What could we do about that?'

- **To gain power**. 'Aha! Tantrums and hitting get me what I want!' No, they don't! We need to look at our own reactions to tantrums and the rewards we might be unwittingly giving. Then determine to ignore her, remove her, and later on, when it's all over, tell her we don't like it.

And of course there are a lot of very normal reasons too, why kids misbehave. They might be tired, hungry or bored. Then they simply need loving parents who can plan well and meet their needs.

Sometimes it will be enough just to keep a tally of the behaviour, for example, 'I'm going to put a cross on this piece of paper every time you two argue. Then I'm going to decide what to do about it.' The children become aware of what they are doing and you won't have to get on your high horse every time. Or you could use it like a chart and arrange a negative consequence at the end of the line.

Disrespectful talk

~

Bearing in mind the ideas in 'Respect for parents', we have a right to expect our children to speak pleasantly to us as we speak with dignity to them.

- ♡ We shouldn't stoop to her level and be abusive back. Remember the traffic officer — he doesn't need to yell and scream to make us respect him. We know he has the power to punish us, even with a charming smile and a warm manner.

- ♡ Speak calmly and respectfully, repeating your request.

- ♡ Tell him your friends don't speak to you like that and neither will he.

- ♡ Tell her you would like to talk when she can communicate in a mature way. In the meantime she can choose where she will go to calm down — the wash house or the garage.

- ♡ Get another adult, preferably the other parent, to back you up and tell him 'not to speak to your mother like that. I don't speak to her like that and neither will you.'

Eating

My children's stomachs seem to have only two levels — starving and full. They are starving all day, until they've had half a mouthful of their dinner, then they are full! Grrrrrrrr!

From 20 months on you could try the following:

♡ Explain that they don't have to finish, but they won't get anything else until the next meal. You decide whether next meal means morning or afternoon tea, or main meal.

♡ Offer 'afters' to those who do finish. It doesn't have to be much — fresh fruit, a handful of nuts or chocolate chips, or a biscuit.

♡ Avoid food one and a half hours before a meal, especially anything with sugar (including juice) or milk. Sugar seems to kill an appetite. Raw vegies are good, if he's threatening to die before tea time.

♡ Put the unfinished meal in the fridge. When she reckons she's hungry again, cheerfully offer the same plate of food, up until the next meal, when she is allowed the new dish. Don't reheat the leftover meal each time. You may have to offer it fifteen times on the first day. Cold food never hurt anyone, unlike salmonella.

♡ If he needs persuasion to get through a piece of toast, cut it into ten or so strips by cutting the toast in half, then cutting each half into five 'soldiers'. Name each strip by his friends, pets or teddies. Then say, 'Oh dear! Don't leave poor Fuzzy out here in the cold. He wants to go in the nice warm tummy with the others.' Or if your child is one of those contrary ones, say, 'Whatever you do, don't eat Fuzzy!'

EATING

♡ Another idea for toast or bread: cut the piece of toast diagonally, then suggest that the child 'eats it into a house' by biting off the two opposite corners. Then make a smaller house, a tiny house and a teeny-weeny house. See what other shapes you can make — a fishing rod, a cricket bat, a moon ...

♡ Make up a story and pause at each mouthful. The story doesn't proceed until the next spoonful is in. 'One morning something dreadful happened ... [mouthful] ... there was a terrible bang ...'

♡ Place a small plastic animal on, say, a pile of mashed potato. Then say, 'Let's see how many mouthfuls you can eat before Dinosaur falls over.'

♡ Explain that our mouths like some food, but our stomachs like other food. Sometimes we let our mouths choose, but once a day (or more) we let our tummies choose. Tummies love vegies, meat and so on. If we don't let our tummies choose sometimes, they get sad and sick.

♡ Remember to bring fun back into mealtimes:
— use candles
— eat on a rug outside
— on a rug inside
— name the food by funny names, such as things that a tyrannosaurus might eat
— take turns eating in each person's bedroom. They must play host, preparing the room and seating people.

EATING

For children under 20 months:

♡ Don't worry too much about food. A baby will never starve itself. Some babies are wonderful eaters and some aren't, and often they begin to eat less after nine months, when they are not growing so much.

♡ Don't spoil a good appetite by forcing him to eat when he's full.

♡ Remember her taste buds will 'grow up', and she will grow into some of the foods she won't eat now.

♡ Give small helpings. Some kids prefer finger foods to spooned-in mush, so they could nibble away on cheese, carrots, cauliflower, bread, cucumber, bananas, pieces of sausage or chicken.

♡ Toddlers need to eat 'little and often' rather than three big meals a day. Give healthy snacks, like fruit, crackers and raw vegies.

♡ Plenty to drink, too. You could leave a drink bottle in a reachable place so he can help himself to water whenever he wants it.

♡ You could ease into the eating up idea by giving praise for finishing a small plateful. As she gets bigger she tries to finish if she has room.

Fighting over toys

Children learn by three different methods:

1. by imitating

2. by being shown and told

3. by trial (I just tried this and it worked).

Therefore when we want to teach them the right way to play, we must:

1. play nicely with them

2. show and tell them how to play nicely

3. reward them for playing nicely — at first anyway. Fair play has its own rewards once you've learned to do it.

♡ To help them learn to share toys we can play with the group for a while, modelling taking turns and so on. Then we leave while everything is sweet, promising to pop back. We come back while they are still playing well so we can praise them. If we wait until chaos sets in before we return, we have actually rewarded bad play.

♡ If a toy is being fought over, remove the toy for three minutes. Then return it quickly so they can have another chance to learn not to argue over it.

♡ Explain that if there is any more fighting then no one has the toy.

♡ Use a timer — five minutes each.

FIGHTING OVER TOYS

- ♡ Let each child tell his side of the story when a problem develops. Kids can feel powerless if they can't appeal to a higher authority. But they will realise they could both lose the toy, and they'll learn to sort out which grizzles are worth bothering you about.

- ♡ If one child is aggressive, remove him to time out.

- ♡ If they are both continually at each other, you could calmly explain: 'I've had enough. I have asked you to speak nicely to each other and you haven't done what I've asked. Jody, you can sweep out the garage; Jamie, you can wash the car.'

- ♡ If one child is continually putting another down, or winning all the battles, try spot checks. Sweep into the room with something yummy 'for the people who are being nice to each other'. Try to come in when they are both good, as well as when your target is not.

- ♡ Food is a great leveller. If the kids have been playing really well but a bit of aggro starts to creep in, try announcing cheerfully, 'Afternoon tea time' or 'Let's make some popcorn.' By the time they have sat and munched for five minutes, they will have forgotten what the difference was about.

Games

Here are some 'different' games, for parties, or just for fun at home.

Balloon chuck

Fill balloons with water. Toss them to each other, moving gradually further apart. Best played outside.

Bombardments

Children form two lines facing each other. Behind each pair of legs is an empty plastic bottle. A small cushion or soft ball is thrown, in an attempt to knock over the other team's bottles. The winner is the last one with their bottle left standing. Have a middle line drawn in chalk.

They may come up to the middle line to throw, but they may not want to leave their bottle unattended. This works best if each team can stand half a metre away from a wall.

Forfeits

Pass a blown-up balloon around a circle. When the music stops the person holding the balloon must sit on it to pop it. Then he must do the action that you have previously written on a piece of paper and placed inside the balloon. Forfeits could be:
— Let everyone sign your tummy.
— Dress up in a net curtain and hum 'Here Comes the Bride' while you walk slowly around the room.
— Eat three crackers then whistle 'Mary Had a Little Lamb'.
— Crawl around the room backwards saying 'Hee-haw'.
— Say 'iced ink' ten times, and so on.

King of the ring

A very rough game. Good for tough kids who are wearing old clothes! Draw, with chalk or paint, a circle on the grass about two metres diameter. All the children pile into the ring. On 'Go' they try to push, shove, drag or pull all the others out of the ring. Once every part of your body is outside the ring, you are out, but then you can pull people from the outside. Last one left in is the winner.

Lolly bob

Hang a wrapped lolly from a string on the clothesline. Children try to grab it in their teeth with their hands behind their backs. Then unwrap it and eat it.

The traditional apple bob in water is not a good idea these days with things like meningitis around.

Round the world

Children sit in a circle. One child is blindfolded and stands in the middle. Going round the circle, each seated child must say the name of a country. When they have all done this, the blindfolded one calls out two countries. The two children who called these must swap seats, while the blindfolded one tries to get to an empty seat first.

Toothpick stack

Give ten to fifteen toothpicks to each child. Everyone has a turn placing one toothpick across the neck of a fizzy bottle. Whoever makes the stack topple must keep all the toothpicks that fall. The winner is the one who gets rid of all their toothpicks first.

High chair high jinks

~

It seems that every baby has to re-invent the law of gravity. 'Look! When I let go my toy, it dwops on the gwound.'

This can be exasperating, but since it's an educational exercise, they are going to learn either 'When it dwops on the gwound, Mummy picks it up' or 'When it dwops on the gwound, it stays there.'

♥ You could leave it there for one minute, then pick it up.

♥ You could sit him on the floor. Babies aged five to eight months who can't yet sit on their own can enjoy sitting in a strong, narrow box or a chilly bin. The sides give him stability and all his toys stay together. It's true! All mine sat in boxes!

♥ If it's the trainer mug she loves to tip upside down, remove it when she is no longer thirsty. Same with a plate of food.

Hitting and biting

~

> Some acts of aggression stem from anger (see 'Dealing with anger') and children need to learn more acceptable ways of expressing their anger. If they keep it up, eventually it will be called assault.

Toddlers try hitting and biting to see if it gets them what they want. They are learning how to relate and solve problems when they don't have much language to help them. They can usually be diverted just before a collision occurs, or gently told, 'Hitting hurts. We don't hit.'

- Or say, 'Biting hurts. We don't bite; we use our mouths for talking. Dogs can't talk; that's why wild dogs bite. But you can tell me how you are feeling and what made you want to bite.' Then use the opportunity to teach verbal strategies: 'I don't like that'; 'Please stop that.'

- If she hits or bites you, you could overreact with a little dramatic presentation. Say how sore it is and that you were going to play with her in the sandpit but now you will have to go and lie down (only for two minutes, though — then into the sandpit, forgiven and forgotten).

- Don't hit or bite back; this only reinforces aggression as a weapon.

- If it is a recurring problem, isolate him in time out. While there, talk about what he has done, and how the other child is feeling.

- Later on you could use the Bunny Principle, to help him see it from the other child's point of view.

HITTING AND BITING

- Monitor the aggression she is watching on television.

- Make sure you are not unknowingly rewarding him in some way for hitting (for example, he gets taken home, where he has you all to himself again).

- You could punish the offending body part: 'Your mouth was naughty to bite Jared, so I'm not going to let your mouth have this yoghurt. Your hands have been very good though, so they can help put the stamps on these letters.'

- If hitting is still a constant problem, you could use one of the ideas in 'Negative charts' on pages 35 and 36.

- Some children bite when they get excited, not really meaning to. A big yell will probably be enough to discourage this. If this happy biting persists, particularly if it is being done to an older child, ask that child to overreact, turning a positive, fun situation into a sad one. The bitten child could say, 'Ow! You bit me! That hurt! I don't want to play with you now.' Explain to your child that you understand she didn't mean to bite, that she just wanted to keep enjoying her friend. But we hug people and bite food. You can't eat your friends, because then you would have no one left to play with! Give both parties something to eat, as a means of regrouping, then they can resume play. Remind her not to bite, but to come to you for a piece of apple if she needs to bite something.

- Don't intervene every time a kid wallops another one, especially if they are both yours! They need to learn how to relate to each other and how to resolve a conflict. Intervene if the aggression is uneven (one is getting hit more), or if it continues.

Holidays

~

Holidays can be wonderful, memory-building adventures. Or they can be disasters.

- ♡ Make sure that you talk about what you, as adults, expect from a holiday. Try to include something for everyone. Adults may like to sleep and read while kids want to go, go, go.

- ♡ Don't let children have too much sugar! Remember that juice and ice blocks are contributing too.

- ♡ Help kids to earn their pocket money before you go. Then they spend their own money instead of nagging for things every day. Jobs might include cleaning the car, vacuuming out the car, sweeping, setting the table, making their bed, raking leaves, cleaning things and so on.

HOLIDAYS

♡ Parents could take turns sleeping in.

♡ Plan to stay at a place where the entertainment is built in, so you won't have to fill every minute of the children's day. Look for a place that:
- is well fenced,
- has a playground,
- has other children,
- has a holiday programme,
- has short walks,
- has an indoor area for wet days.

♡ Take fine weather toys (buckets and spades) and wet weather toys (Lego and colouring books).

♡ Save your best ideas for later in the holiday, instead of doing all the fun things first.

♡ See the ideas in 'Car travel'.

'I'm bored'

Don't you just love those words?

My kids know that I have a list of 'things you can do when I hear you say there's nothing to do'. The list goes something like this:
- clean windows
- sweep cobwebs
- clean garage
- pick up cabbage leaves
- sweep paths
- wash car
- dusting
- tidy bedroom
- and so on.

To be fair, I sit down with them, especially at the start of the holidays, and together we make lists of things they could enjoy doing, so they won't need to come and tell me they are bored.

Things to do by myself

- puzzles
- reading
- Lego
- write a letter
- bike ride
- play on trampoline/swing
- sandpit
- colouring in
- hopscotch

Things to do with my brother

- board games
- cricket
- golf
- have catches
- make a hut
- skipping
- climb trees
- woodwork
- dig for treasure
- chalk murals
- make a treasure hunt
- tennis on wall

Things to do with Mum (once a day)

- go for a walk
- make a craft
- have a card game
- baking

Here's an idea for someone who still thinks they are bored: sort the hundreds and thousands into their colours; or get all the letters out of the soup mix and make your name.

Learning to talk

Babies start to learn to talk with the first gooey sounds they make. Some seem to speak fluently in a foreign language soon after, and some don't speak English until much later. Most children just seem to 'pick up' language, but we can do a lot to help them develop a rich and clear vocabulary.

- ♡ Talk to her all the time (within reason), even when she is a tiny baby.

- ♡ Name objects around the house. Describe what you are doing.

- ♡ Where possible, have eye contact when you talk.

- ♡ Emphasise a noun: 'Oh look, there's a truck. Truck.'

- ♡ Give praise for words attempted, then say the word correctly. 'Oh, ruck ... yes, that's right, it's a truck.' Don't criticise or laugh at incorrect attempts.

- ♡ Look at books, naming the things in the pictures, asking him, 'Where's the dog?' and so on. Read the captions too. Make the noises of animals, fire engines and trains as you read about them to babies. Rhymes and nursery rhymes are great too.

- ♡ Extend her language. When she picks up a block and says 'Block', say 'Yes, block. That's a yellow block. And here's a green block.'

- ♡ Singing and dancing also help to develop language, and a sense of rhythm.

LEARNING TO TALK

- ♡ Give him time to get his answer or explanation out. Don't rush in too quickly and supply the words for him.

- ♡ These days it's getting harder to find time to talk to our kids, and we're relying more and more on the television and the computer to do our communicating for us. But there is no substitute for live language. Without an oral vocabulary children will have trouble learning to read. They can't learn to read the word if they don't know the word exists.

Leaving your child with someone else

This can be traumatic for you, and your child, but it's very important to do it because:

▲ children need other people in their lives

▲ they need to learn to trust other people and to feel safe away from you

▲ they can begin to form their own special relationships with grandparents, and other adults

▲ you need a break; maybe not now, but you need to set a pattern so that you can take a break later and not be so worried and guilty that you can't enjoy yourself.

A few things to remember:

♡ Make sure you have complete confidence in the person you are leaving him with.

♡ Express this confidence to him.

♡ Don't let him see your doubts and insecurities about this.

♡ Explain what is happening, how long you will be away, and that you will come back.

♡ When it is time to go, don't sneak out, but say goodbye to her, even if it makes her cry. If you don't, she will never know at what moment of the day you might walk out on her and she will be more insecure.

- ♡ You could let her have a small treat when you are gone.

- ♡ Remind yourself that he will be fine. He probably stopped crying once your car was out of the driveway. Even if he didn't, he won't suffer any permanent psychological harm just because you went to the pictures.

So have a good time. You deserve it!

Returning to work

You've thought about it long and hard. You know that the only place you are truly indispensable is in your child's life. You know your child needs you more than any other person, and that no one can parent him as well as you can. But a situation is presenting itself in which you will have to be away from him for longer than you would like.

There are several things you can do to make this situation easier for all of you.

- ♡ Try to make the time you do have together fun, happy and memorable. It might be worth spending the extra dollars employing a housekeeper so you can enjoy Saturdays together, or have weekends away.

- ♡ If meal preparation is started for you, you can have some precious minutes together at the end of the day, before you need to begin rushing again. Or you might be able to let your child help to peel potatoes or wash carrots.

- ♡ Having a bath or shower can be fun — you need to do it anyway, so why not together?

- ♡ If you give your kids the first five minutes you are in the door (Dads especially), they will leave you alone for more of the evening. You could draw a picture together about your days, do some colouring in and chat, romp on the floor, play a game outside …

LEAVING YOUR CHILD WITH SOMEONE ELSE

♡ Try to find an opportunity to show your kids where you work, so they will have an understanding of what you are doing while they are waiting for you to return.

♡ Tell them about your day, as well as asking about theirs.

♡ Instead of feeling guilty about the time apart, make the time together count!

When looking for longer-term daycare there are basically three options, and you need to choose the one that best suits you.

1 Have someone in your home.

2 Take your child to a caregiver's home.

3 Various forms of daycare centre.

Let's look at the pros and cons of each of these.

A caregiver in your home

Advantages:
— You don't have to wake your child on cold winter mornings.
— It's quicker for you in the mornings; no dropping off.
— It's more settled for a small baby: same room, bed and so on.
— The job can include some housework and meal preparation.

Disadvantages:
— Probably the most expensive option.
— It's an invasion of your privacy to have someone else in your home.
— There may be no one else to keep an eye on the caregiver, or help in an emergency. You must choose someone you trust implicitly.
— It could be a long, lonely day for the caregiver.

LEAVING YOUR CHILD WITH SOMEONE ELSE

2 A caregiver's home

Advantages:
— More interesting for an older child, especially if there are other children. They get to come home later.
— It may be closer and handier than a daycare centre. If you live in the country, leaving the child at a neighbour's place can mean you can be flexible and include him in farm activities when it suits.
— If you are held up late in the day, the hours may be more flexible than a centre. Perhaps she could even bed down at the caregiver's place.
— Your child can become part of the caregiver's day: going to the gym, shopping and so on, in a natural setting.

Disadvantages:
— You still have to drop the child off.
— When the caregiver is unavailable owing to sickness and so on, it's your job to find a replacement.
— They may be more fussy than you are about what your child touches and so on.
— You may have to employ another person to do the housework. (Perhaps the caregiver could come to your place one morning a week.)

3 Daycare centres

Advantages:
— Probably the cheapest of the three.
— The staff are trained in childcare.
— For an older child, there is the company of other children and a greater variety of activities.
— There is usually a well set up, safe outdoor and indoor facility.

LEAVING YOUR CHILD WITH SOMEONE ELSE

Disadvantages:
— More time out of your day to drop her off.
— You have no control over the others who attend. Your darling may have to spend eight hours a day in the company of a monster.
— You have no say in the staff who are employed there.
— It could have less of a family atmosphere than the other two options.

Whether you employ an individual or an institution, these are some of the things you might want to look into before you make the decision:

♡ Up-to-date first aid, especially CPR.

♡ A happy, busy atmosphere. You could visit the home or centre at its busiest time, possibly just before lunch. If your interest and observation are not welcome, question that too!

♡ Policies that agree with yours, for example for dealing with an unsettled child, a tantrum or misbehaviour.

♡ What written or verbal feedback is available about the child's day?

♡ Is there an adequate sleep area for under twos?

♡ What is the ratio of staff to children?

♡ Are the standards of behaviour the same as or higher than yours at home? If he is allowed to walk around eating at Auntie Jean's place, then he'll want to do it at home. If Auntie Jean is quite strict you can always slacken off at home, but it's no fun having to tighten up at home, especially after a long day at work.

♡ If your child is likely to use this situation for several years, is there an extension programme to keep her interest up as she gets older? Is there a transition programme to help with the move to school?

♡ If you're looking to employ an individual you may want to know about their maturity, experience, ability to have fun, to cope in a crisis, and to cope with clinginess, tantrums, sickness and so on.

Making friends

~

Making friends seems to be something some kids do without even trying, while others don't know where to start. These kids might need to be deliberately taught some of the skills that go with making and being friends.

To teach these skills, use role-plays with people and teddies, use stories, and just plain talk about it.

♡ Saying hello. Learn to look at the person and say their name.

♡ Asking someone to play with you. Have a game in mind already, for example, 'Do you want to play rugby with me?' rather than just 'Do you want to play with me?'

♡ Replying to a question. Here's an object lesson: Say to your child that you are going to teach him a new ball game. You will throw him three balls which he must hold and not return. Say, 'That wasn't much of a game, was it?' Then explain how conversation can be like this. Someone throws you a question, trying to open a conversation, but you give a one-word answer; you don't return the conversation to them. Not much of a game; not much of a conversation. If someone says, 'How is school, Jason?', most kids reply in one word: 'Okay', 'Good', 'Rotten.' Practise 'throwing the balls back'. 'Good, thanks. We're going to the museum next week to look at the spider display' or 'Terrible. It's so boring and we're not allowed to use the PE gear at lunchtime.' Practise talking as you throw the balls back and forth.

MAKING FRIENDS

- Not interrupting. Waiting for a break in the traffic before you add your bit.

- Playing something you don't want to; not always getting your own choice, but participating anyway.

- Sharing.

- Taking turns.

- Following rules.

- Reaching a compromise. Encountering rules you don't agree with, or haven't met before (or people in the same categories); putting up with them anyway.

- Being able to say 'No' to silly, dangerous or inappropriate ideas put forward by the group. To be able to say why you don't like it and suggest something else.

- Being able to suggest a game. Have some ideas in your head.

  If a school-aged child is having a hard time keeping friends, you may have to look at why.

- Is he 'different' in some way? You may be able to do something about it. Perhaps clothes, skin care, glasses frames and so on could make the difference. Or helping him cope with shyness, giftedness or a disability.

- Is everyone else different? Then she probably doesn't want to fit in, and perhaps you don't want her to either. These just aren't her type of people. In this case she will just need plenty of support at home, and fun with peers in other contexts, until she eventually finds herself, maybe at high school, with like-minded people. (Be careful of using this as an excuse, though. We would all like to think that our kids are perfect. Try to see her as the other children see her.)

MAKING FRIENDS

♡ Is he doing things that would annoy the other children? Picking his nose, being bossy, chewing loudly, criticising people, complaining, not following rules, talking too much, getting huffy about losing a game, being aggressive, telling on other children, bragging, being a know-all or wanting to be in charge of everything? Try to identify the problem behaviours, talk about the effect they are having, and practise the opposite.

> For more help on this see *Nobody Likes Me: Helping Your Child Make Friends* by Elaine McEwan.

Messy play

♡ Try to let the kids have access to the whole house and not to have 'don't touch' areas which will only stress you unnecessarily. Simply move the breakable and dangerous things higher up. You can use clips to hold some cupboards shut, but leave at least one that he can get into — maybe where you keep pots and lids, plastic containers or bowls. Believe it or not, hauling all this stuff out and making a dreadful din with it is actually developing his brain. There are five gates into a child's brain — eyes, ears, nose, mouth and touch: the five senses. The more tactile or touching experiences a child has, the more memorable an experience is and the more he learns and remembers. So keep squishing, pouring, sloshing and squeezing.

♡ Water play is great development too. Let her play in the sink with plastic utensils, funnel, jug, cups and so on. You could add cold water after you have done the dishes — the bubbles are fun too. It doesn't take long to dry the floor at the end — use a big towel then throw it in the washing machine.

♡ Make an apron from those thick, plastic pet food bags. The plastic doesn't bend or cling so isn't dangerous. Cut holes for the head and arms.

♡ When baking, choose recipes with lots of stirring, shaping and squishing to get the most out of the exercise, things like cheese biscuits, bread, Belgium biscuits and pastries.

♡ It may seem as though you spend all day cleaning up messes, but honestly, this stage doesn't last long.

MESSY PLAY

- Maybe you could have just one (or two) good tidy-ups a day; perhaps when they are all in bed.

- Finger painting.
    - Mix together in a pot ½ cup cornflour, ¼ cup cold water and a trickle of food colouring. Add 2½ cups boiling water. Mix well, then leave to set for ten minutes.
    - To use finger paint, put a little in a sponge roll tin or another shallow container with sides, or on a piece of plastic outside. The child swishes and swirls until she has made her perfect picture, then you can lie a piece of paper across the painting, pat lightly, then remove.

- What about toe painting? Outside, of course!

- Put a bucket or baby bath of water outside, or a paddling pool. Leave plastic cups, jugs, funnels and so on. Please stay to supervise.

- Water in the sandpit is great fun, to make rivers, lakes and a mess. (Rinse the clothes before you put them in the washing machine this time. Electricians hate pumps full of sand.)

- There are lots of things apart from brushes you can use for painting. Try sponges, feathers, balls, rocks, leaves and so on.

- For a water slide, buy five or six metres of polythene from a garden shop — much cheaper than a commercial slide.

> **Don't feel guilty if you're not in the mood for messy play today. Simply divert to a quiet, clean game and wait for another day when you've had more sleep, the sun is shining, and you feel more able to cope with the mess.**

Nagging

'Can I have a horse?' 'No!'
'Can I have a horse?' 'No!'
'Can I have a horse?' 'No!'
'Can I have a horse?' 'No!'
'Can I have a horse?' 'Oh, all right!'

If our kids nag a lot, we may need to ask ourselves, Have I trained her that nagging eventually works?

- First we must train ourselves that 'No' means no.

- Then we can train our child that 'No' means no.

- Say, 'I said "No, you can't." That means no matter how many times you ask, you still can't. Please don't ask again.'

- Make a game out of nagging. Say, 'Okay. You've got five minutes to tell me all the reasons why you should have a horse. You are not allowed to say "Um" or stop. Ready? Go!' If everyone in the family has a different request they could all talk at once, once a day.

- When you turn down a request, give your child the dignity of a legitimate reason, not just 'Because I said so.' For example, 'You can't have a horse because they cost $500 and we have only $40 spare this week. We don't have a paddock to keep it in and …'

- Count to five before you answer a child's request. This tells him that you are considering what he has asked for. It also gives you time to either realise you could manage this one or put into words why you couldn't.

NAGGING

♡ Try to say 'Yes' to the things requiring your time, but in a way that you can cope with: 'Sure, I'd love to play cricket with you. Let's have ten minutes after tea.' This could well be the quality time that fills her emotional tank and leaves her contented, not needing to nag.

♡ When he nags for material things, like lollies at the supermarket, you could:
— say you might buy a lolly, but only on the days that he doesn't ask
— have a lolly jar at home; give a lolly to people who didn't ask, when you get home
— make a joke of it by saying 'Nag, nag, nag' in your best fisherman's wife voice
— praise him for not nagging. Perhaps when he is just puckering up his face for a good whine, you jump in with 'Thank you for not nagging and waiting quietly while I talk to Mrs Smith.'

♡ Give him a system for saving up for something he wants — chores, graphs of money earned and so on.

♡ A response to 'When can we go swimming?' might be 'Ten minutes after you stop nagging!'

New baby

There will always be sibling rivalry, as long as siblings are human. But we can minimise the trauma that little Brad feels when the new baby comes home. Suddenly he is knocked from his perch and is no longer the youngest in the family with Mum and Dad's attention all to himself.

- ♡ Warn him. There's a baby coming! The baby-in-the-tummy is a difficult concept for a littlie, and before you know it everyone's got babies in their tummies. But he can understand getting the room ready for the baby that is coming to live in the family.

- ♡ Let him help to set up the crib and get the clothes ready.

- ♡ When shopping for the baby, let him choose something. Involve him in decision making.

- ♡ After the baby is brought home, let him hold her, play with her and bring toys for her to look at. Allow him to develop his own relationship with her.

- ♡ Tell him that she loves watching her big brother and all the clever things he can do. Prop her up where she can see him and thank him for helping to keep her amused.

- ♡ Use the phrases 'your sister' and 'our baby'.

- ♡ When she cries and you are busy with Brad, call out, 'Hang on, Baby. You'll have to wait. I'm helping Brad at the moment.' This gives him the message that he is still very important and Baby doesn't always come first. He'll probably give you a big grin and call out, 'Yeah, Baby. Mum's helping me at the moment.'

♡ When visitors fuss over the baby, try to involve Brad in the fuss by letting him tell her name and so on, and by focusing on his achievements this week, or showing the artwork he has done.

♡ Save a favourite activity for times when you are going to be busy with the baby. My kids loved to play in the sink, so I only let them do this when I was breastfeeding the baby. Before I settled down to feed, I would fill up the sink, maybe add bubbles, put out plastic cups, jug and funnels, and put a thick plastic apron on the child (see 'Messy play'). I stayed in the same room so we could chat as he puddled.

♡ Other ideas for this favourite activity might be playdough (see recipe below), painting, ringing a friend or grandparent, puzzles, colouring, blocks or Duplo. Let him continue past the crisis time if he is absorbed, but pack it all away when he wanders off.

Playdough recipe
2 cups flour
2 cups water
½ cup salt
2 tsp cream of tartar
2 Tbsp oil
food colouring

Combine all the ingredients in a heavy-based pot. Cook over a low heat, stirring until the mixture leaves the sides of the pot and there is a colour change. Cool before using. Store in covered containers or plastic bags in the fridge.

♡ Some people buy a special bathable doll for their child and present it when the new baby comes home. Then the older child can look after her baby while you look after yours.

Pocket money

There are many good reasons for giving children pocket money, even just a little bit:

♡ They learn the value of money, the agony of money spent unwisely, and how to spend wisely.

♡ They learn to count money.

♡ You can redirect their nagging for things into saving up and deciding what they really want.

♡ It gives us, as adults, something to deduct when we feel the need.

♡ We can reward them for extra tasks done and the attitude with which they are done.

♡ Pocket money gives children a sense of responsibility, and in a small way, of power, thus improving their self-esteem.

Younger children

A chart system is probably best for three- to six-year-olds (see 'Charts').

Stars can be awarded for doing what they are told, obeying first time, showing initiative and completing set chores.

✱	✱	✱	✱	✱			30c that week
✱	✱	✱	✱	✱	✱	✱	45c that week

To award the pocket money, you can:

— give her the set amount, say 50 cents, as soon as she completes a line, or
— treat each line as a week. At the end of the week, award five or ten cents for every star on that line.

Older children

For ages six to eight you could use the chart where ticks are given for specific tasks (see 'Charts').

After eight to ten years a set amount is probably best, as they might start to expect to be paid for every little thing they are asked to do. The amount can be reduced as they fail to fulfil expected obligations, like cleaning their room.

You could negotiate with her at the beginning of the year. 'Now that you are nine, you should be getting $2 pocket money a week, providing that you clean your room on Saturday, feed the dog every day [and so on]. However, if you also vacuum the lounge and wash the car I will give you $5. You choose.'

Potty training

Potty training is very easy when he is ready and very hard when he is not. Here are a few ideas to try:

♡ Dabble in potty training for three days. If it's not working, leave it for a month, then try again for another three days.

♡ Leave the potty in a prominent place. Let her use it as a seat, a hat, whatever.

♡ Let him run around in just undies (off the carpet). When he wets say, 'Oh look! You've done wees. That would be better in the potty.' Better still, catch him mid trickle and put him on the potty, so a bit goes in. Then make a big fuss with lots of praise. Maybe leave the trophy to show Daddy when he gets home. This is easier in summer.

♡ Never scold for failures, but praise for success.

♡ Let her see you going to the toilet.

For further help, see *Pyjamas Don't Matter* by Trish Gribben.

Shyness

I tell my kids, 'Shyness is a luxury we can't afford.' I would love to be shy — I wouldn't have to meet new people, or work at relationships. But my life, and theirs, are richer because we don't allow ourselves to be shy.

All babies go through a shy stage, but most of them come through it if:

- ▲ we expect them to come through it
- ▲ we continue to take them out and mix with people
- ▲ we don't offer them an excuse: 'Oh, she's shy.'

Some ideas:

- ♥ We can teach children how to say hello to people: 'When Mrs Jones says hello to you, look her in the eye, then say, "Hello, Mrs Jones."'

- ♥ Role-play this at home to practise. Use people and teddies.

- ♥ Role-play asking another child to play, or being asked to play. What will you say? What did Teddy say? Did Fluffy like it when he looked away and said nothing?

- ♥ When a new teddy or doll comes into the house, one of the other toys can introduce him to the others, ask him his name and if he wants to play. Or New Ted could introduce himself if no one is making a move. Practise social behaviour and have fun at the same time.

Spoiling children

It's impossible to define spoiling. In one street the spoilt kid is the one with shoes and laces, while in another street it's the kid with three swimming pools. In our overindulged Western society, it could be safe to say that our kids are spoilt when they have as much as, or more than, the other kids in their orbit.

There are two main reasons why we shouldn't spoil our kids with 'things':

1. We actually rob them of pleasure by giving them too much. What is a drink, without thirst? Remember the first time you went on a hydroslide? It wouldn't be that good if you went every day, would it?

2. If he gets something before he really wants it, then he doesn't have the excitement of hope and expectation, or the pleasure of receiving.

So ... how much is too much?
I hate it when people answer a question with a question, but ...

▲ How long has she wanted this?

▲ How long since she wanted something else this badly?

▲ How much did he appreciate (and how long did he play with) the last thing I gave him?

SPOILING CHILDREN

♡ My daughter is one of those kids who desperately wants 'just one last thing' and she would be eternally happy if only she had it. I usually say, 'Is this the only thing in the world that you really want? Well, if it's still the only thing at Christmas time, I'll think about it.'

♡ Children under three don't need a lot of toys. They can have fun stacking margarine containers, playing in sand or water, and making huts out of chairs and a blanket. Our all-time favourite outside toy has been the sandpit, and the inside one would be the stairs.

♡ Beyond three years I personally feel that our children will appreciate gifts more if we don't give them very often. Apart from Christmas and birthday and having their own pocket money, one or two other gifts a year is plenty.

♡ We also need to remember that whatever we do this year becomes an expectation for next year. It is easy to find appealing, cheap toys for small children, but it costs many more dollars to achieve the same appeal for an older child. Be careful not to give yourself a hard act to follow!

Sulking

Sometimes children learn to capitalise on an emotion to get results. Anger that turns into manipulation is a tantrum. Sadness that is used to manipulate is sulking.

To get the best mileage out of a good sulk, you've got to not let on what you're sulking about.
'What's the matter, honey?'
'Nuffin'.'
'Are you upset about the TV?'
'Hmmph.'
'The tea I cooked?'
'Hmmph.'
And on it goes. We actually reward the sulking by asking all these questions, and allowing the child to inconvenience us.
We also teach them that if you want attention, be miserable! Know any adults that do that?

♡ A better approach might be: 'Honey, I love you and I want to help. I'll be in the garden. Come and tell me what it is you want.'

♡ Sulking without an audience soon shrivels up and dies.

♡ If you can see a sulk coming, whip the carpet out from under her with a comment like: 'You might like to get your dagger eyes ready, because I'm about to ask you to help me with the dishes.' This really unsettles the actress!

Swearing

> It's great to be able to say to your kids, 'You can do and say anything you see and hear me do and say.'
> Be a role model!

♡ Little kids will hear a word and try it out. Don't hit the roof. Say, 'That's a bad word. We don't use that word.' Let them ask you about new words, to see if they are bad or not. My son heard 'pimp squeaks' at school and thought it must be very naughty. Explain some of the meanings of the words, where appropriate.

♡ If he persists, knowing you don't like it, ask him to leave the room, and say, 'I will enjoy talking to you when you can talk to me in a pleasant and mature way' or 'Your mouth isn't a rubbish dump. Don't put rubbish like that into it.'

♡ After she has calmed down, explain that people use these words because they feel powerless to express themselves in any other way. It's like hitting your head against a wall — you only hurt yourself. People will think less of you when they hear you talking like this.

♡ Set boundaries: every time he uses that word (or a repeated put-down phrase), he has to
— give ten cents to the person he said it to
— clean the shoes of the person he said it to
— be the slave for ten minutes of the person he said it to
— lose ten cents from his weekly pocket money
— make a paper flower for the person he said it to (something ridiculous helps to relieve the tension).

♡ You could use a negative chart (see 'Charts') if the problem persists.

Television and computers

Yes, the big one — TV! How much should kids watch? How long should they play on the computer? What censor rating should we let them see? Can he have a television in his room? This is a very controversial area, and one in which every family must make its own decisions.

- ♡ It's a good idea to watch television together occasionally. This tells your child that you are interested in what interests her. Get her to tell you about the characters and the plot. She'll be chuffed at your involvement, and you'll be able to see if it's suitable at the same time. Similarly, ask her to teach you one of her computer games.

- ♡ Keep alert for signs of copycat violence in young children. You may want to restrict or eliminate some programmes or games.

♡ Ask questions about the programmes or games:
  — What behaviours are these actors displaying?
  — What is the language like? (It may not necessarily be swearing, just slovenly, unimaginative gossip.)
  — What values is it portraying?

Research into television and computer involvement seems to suggest that these activities stifle children's imagination and creativity. This makes sense when you consider that watching TV uses only two of the five senses, but climbing a tree or building a hut involves all of them. Educationally children are better off playing than watching. I've even heard one teacher say she would rather see children fighting than watching TV! And yes, she is a mother too!

Telling tales

> Children feel powerless a lot of the time. Life in the playground can be like the animal kingdom where the toughest and biggest survive. They need to be able to appeal to a higher authority. Let them tell you what's going on.

Often children can't distinguish between a tale and a problem, but we can field the calls and decide which ones to follow up on. I'd rather listen to a hundred 'tales' I didn't need to know, than miss the one about Sam and the matches in the haybarn.

I also suspect that if she knows she can come to me any time, she will feel more secure and won't need to come.

- Ask, 'What can I do to help?'

- Ask, 'What can *you* do to help?'

- Teach him to say, 'I don't like that. Please stop that.'

- Teach him to walk away and play with someone else.

- If you suspect that the taleteller is just as much at fault, for example for squabbling, then inconvenience both parties. Put the toy away or make each child sit on the grass for three minutes. Gradually it will dawn on the taleteller that sometimes it's better to sort things out yourself.

Trips

≈

The pressure is always on to go out and spend money. But we can build wonderful memories in places that didn't cost a cent.

The beach

♡ In winter, forget the togs, but take spades, buckets, a frisbee or ball, vinegar and baking soda (see making volcanoes below). Climb on the rocks, make huge lying-down dinosaurs on the sand. Make sandcastles — don't forget the moat, the forest where the dragon lives, the flags, the tower where the wicked stepsister has been locked up for sixty years, the horses' stable and the knights' quarters.

♡ Make volcanoes. Build a mound about 20 cm high. Push your hand down into it to make a hollow. Put a heaped teaspoon of baking soda down the hole. Now add one tablespoon of vinegar and watch your volcano erupt!

♡ Collect crabs from under rocks. Take them up the beach, draw a start line and a finish line, then have a crab race. Put the crabs back.

♡ Collect shells. At home stick them to cardboard with PVA to make a picture, or cover a plastic plant pot with Polyfilla and push the shells into the plaster.

♡ Have races on the sand — running, hopping, jumping, three-legged (cut sections of a tyre tube, or make rings of elastic, for joining legs).

- See how many different live things you can find in a rock pool. How many can you name?

A playground

- Grab another family and have a game of softball, cricket, T-Ball or soccer.
- Take roller blades and skateboards to a large concrete area.

Lookout

If you have a lookout in your area, take a map and try to locate different landmarks, suburbs and so on.

Wet picnic

Try to think of a place in your area where you could have a 'picnic in the rain', for example a band rotunda, old battlements, a large culvert and so on. Children love an eccentric parent! (Well, even if they hate it, they'll be glad to get home again!)

Wetlands and bush

Take binoculars, magnifying glass, specimen jars, and any books about birds and insects you can borrow.

Visit a farm

Wear old clothes and gumboots.

Then of course there's always the museum, art gallery, a cathedral, a local cemetery even, and scenic walks and drives. Try to think like a tourist in your own town and discover the places you take for granted.

*W*aking too early
in the morning

~

Some children need less sleep than others and wake up when it still feels like the middle of the night for the rest of us.

Some kids will sleep longer in the morning if we cut out a day sleep, or put them to bed later, or sew black-out lining on the curtains or hang a thick rug over the window. Otherwise we can't make kids sleep longer than their little inside clocks are telling them, but we can encourage them to play quietly in their rooms until 6:30.

- Make a special morning area, perhaps a little table. Leave a snack — carrot sticks, dry cornflakes, dried fruit and so on. Provide crayons and paper, books and soft toys. Even if this stalls her for only two minutes, she is beginning to learn a good habit.

- Leave out two piles of clothes. He can choose which pile to put on.

- An older child could have a digital clock in her room. You could stick a piece of paper over the minutes, so she can only see the number showing the hour. Then you can say, 'You can get up when this number is a six.'

- The alarm could be set on 'Radio' so that he is allowed to get up when the music starts.

Waking up in the night

~

By the time babies are nine months old, they probably don't need to be fed during the night. If we are sure they don't actually need anything, we can take steps to break their habit of waking in the night.

♡ Make sure he has a full tummy and an empty bladder (non nappy wearers) when he goes to bed.

♡ Older children could keep a safety sip drink bottle on a chair beside the bed.

♡ If she is a blanket rejecter, dress her in warm but light clothes and use a panel heater with a reliable thermostat set at about 15°C. Do not dress babies under nine months in bulky clothes as this can increase the risk of cot death.

♡ Now get ready to have nerves of steel and ignore some crying for a few nights. I know it's quicker and easier to get up and deal with it than to lie awake listening to the noise, but it's worth it in the long run. Perhaps shift the cot to the furthest but safest (and warm) part of the house from your bedroom.

♡ Crying is his most powerful weapon to get you to change your behaviour. You may have been rewarding him up until now, but it's time to change. At present his little mind is thinking, 'Hello. I'm awake. I will cry and Mum will come with cuddles and a warm drink and soft words.' What we want him to think is, 'Hello. I'm awake. I shall roll over and go back to sleep.' He can't begin to change until we stop rewarding him for waking up! Remind yourself it is just a habit and habits can be changed.

♡ Reassure yourself that this baby has a greater need. More than to see you, she needs a good night's sleep and a well-rested parent!

So ... what you do when he cries is this: don't get up!

This really is the best way, but if you just can't manage to go cold turkey, then make yourself wait ten minutes, then go in, hopefully when there is a lull in the crying. In a robotic fashion, pick him up, cuddle him long enough for him to settle, pop him back in bed, then leave. This time wait fifteen minutes, the next time 20 minutes and so on.

It is easier if you do something during these waiting minutes instead of just wringing your hands — take a walk in the garden, visit the car in the garage, play with the dog in the backyard, listen to the stereo.

For an older child, if she gets out of bed and comes to see you, then don't say anything (warm conversation is a reward), take her firmly by the hand and lead her quietly back to bed.

For more help with this, see *The Sleep Book* by Kathy MacDonald.

What teachers wish new entrants knew

What things are most important for a five-year-old to know when he arrives at school? I asked ten teachers from seven different schools to help me answer this question.

They were given a list of sixteen skills that five-year-olds can and cannot do, and were asked to rate these skills in order of importance. While they all agreed that all the skills are important, the skills came out in this order, with the most important being at the top.

1. Able to toilet themselves.
2. Confident to be away from parents.
3. Able to control anger, not be violent.
4. Be accustomed to and confident with conversation.
5. Able to share.
6. Have a large oral vocabulary.
7. Able to write their name.
8. Having an understanding of personal space.
9. Able to blow their nose.
10. Know strategies for dealing with things they don't like. (For example, 'I don't like that', moving away and so on.)

11 Able to count to ten.

12 Know the names of letters.

13 Know the sounds of letters.

14 Know colours.

15 Know some of the children in the class.

16 Able to tie their shoes.

Some of the teachers also added to their list things like:
- able to listen to instructions
- able to dress themselves (after swimming, jackets on after school)
- manners, including not interrupting
- looking after their own gear
- respect for others and property
- able to cope with a packed lunch
- able to clean up after themselves
- having a positive attitude to school and learning
- able to sit on the mat without fidgeting
- able to take risks ('I could say something, but I might be wrong')
- able to recognise their name written down.

It might help to be aware of one or two areas that are high up on the list, in which your child is less confident. Then try, in a fun way, to put yourselves in situations where you can work on these together.

Whining or baby talk

♡ First we must make sure that we are not rewarding her for a whiny voice, by tuning out her chatter in a normal voice and only responding when she uses the whine. Try to tune in to the normal voice by responding to it, and not responding to the baby voice or grizzle.

♡ For baby talk, say, 'Hang on, that's not Samantha's voice. It's Samantha I love, so I want to hear what Samantha has to say.'

♡ For whining, explain that you don't like that talk and you are going to ignore it. For very little children you could say, 'I can't hear you when you talk in that voice.' Tell him you want to hear what he is saying, but if you seem not to hear him, it is because you are ignoring that tone of voice.

♡ You could use a negative chart (see 'Charts').

Crafty ideas for preschoolers

Balloon yo-yos

You will need:
- a balloon
- some sand or soil
- 5–10 rubber bands.

Use a funnel to fill the balloon with half a cup of sand. Tie a knot in the balloon, and as you do this, include one of the rubber bands in the knot, so it is attached to the balloon. Now fold the second rubber band in half and put it inside the first. Push one folded end inside the other folded end, then pull it tight. You now have two bands joined. Keep joining rubber bands until they are the right length for the height of your child. There you are! A yo-yo! Teenagers love these too!

Blocks

To get more mileage from your interconnecting blocks like Duplo, try these games.

 Sit back to back so you can't see what the other person is doing. Now the adult builds a small tower of about six different-coloured blocks. Without showing the child, tell her what you have made, describing the order and colours. She builds one the same. Then compare and see how you got on. This is great for listening skills, learning colours and following instructions.

♡ Same again, but the child builds first and describes.

♡ Build a simple something, then put a pillowcase or tablecloth over it. The child has to build a replica by feeling it.

Boats

You will need:
    a plastic soft drink bottle
    a bread knife and board to cut it with
    playdough
    magazines.

Cut the bottle in half lengthways. Put some playdough in one half. Cut animals or people from magazines and make them stand up in the playdough.

You could use a margarine lid instead of a bottle.

Try it in the bath.

Bones

You will need:
    chicken bones
    PVA glue
    sand
    a paintbrush.

After you have eaten the roast chicken, boil up the bones until they are separated and clean. (You could make soup out of the water.) Make a cement out of sand and PVA glue. Now encourage your budding palaeontologist to reconstruct the bird, or invent a new one, by gluing the bones together using the paintbrush.

Bookends

You will need:
> 2 shampoo bottles with screw-on lids
> sand or soil
> cardboard and scissors
> paint.

Fill two old shampoo bottles with sand or soil. Before you put the lid on, cut a circle of cardboard, about 6 cm diameter. This is the hat. Cut a circle from the centre, the size of the lid. Slip the hat on, then screw on the lid. Then paint a face and clothes onto the bottle.

Chalk hopscotch

You will need:
> chalk
> a stone.

In case you've forgotten how it goes, draw large squares, big enough to stand in, like this:

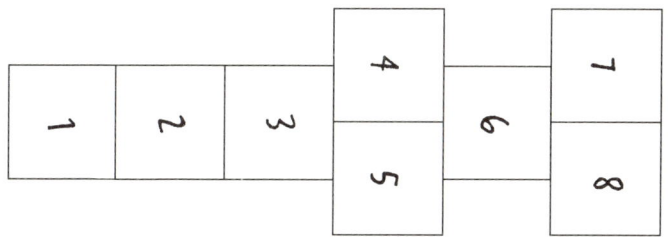

The rules:
> Throw a small stone into square 1.
> Hop right over this square, landing on one foot in square 2.
> Continue hopping into 3, both feet down in 4 and 5, hop to 6,
>   both feet down in 7 and 8.
> Now jump around 180°, so your left foot is now in 8 and you are
>   facing back down the squares.

Hop to 6, two feet for 4 and 5, hop to 3 then 2.
Now pick up your stone in square 1, hop in that square, then out.
Now throw your stone into square 2.
Hop to 1, then 3 and continue.

If your foot goes over a line, or the stone doesn't go into the right square, it is the other person's turn.

Dump trucks

You will need:
- trucks and cars
- horse chestnuts, tiny cones, nuts, pebbles or polystyrene packaging.

To allow your kids to use their trucks inside on a wet day, use any of the above ideas. Let him use the vacuum cleaner when he has finished.

Farms

Make a model of a farm by using the following:
- a sponge roll tin to arrange it all in
- coconut mixed with green food colouring for the grass
- plastic animals, trees, fences, people, vehicles and a small house
- a circle of tinfoil for the pond
- a strip of blue material or cloth for the river
- a teaspoon to eat the coconut as you go!

Feeding birds

You will need:
- a milk carton, scissors and string
- breadcrumbs or fat.

Make a bird feeding tray by cutting out the two opposite sides of a milk carton. Punch a hole in the top and hang it in a tree with string. Place breadcrumbs or fat inside for the birds.

Or make fat balls for birds.

You will need:
   a small (yoghurt) pottle
   fat
   onion bag material.

Pour liquid fat, slightly cooled, into the pottle. When it has set, tip it out and wrap it in some onion bag material. Tie it at the top and hang it in a tree.

Flax baskets

You will need:
   7 strips of flax, about 60 cm long
   knife or scissors to cut them.

Place three strips of flax horizontally, next to each other. Lay the fourth vertically, across the top of the three. Lift up the middle one of the three, to place the vertical one under it, thus 'weaving' it (1). Take the fifth strip of flax. Weave it in vertically also, by lifting the first and third horizontal strips, so it goes 'under, over, under'. The sixth strip will be 'over, under, over' (2).

Now cut four thin strips from the last piece of flax, about 5 mm wide. Use these to tie all four ends, about 15 cm from the weaving (3).

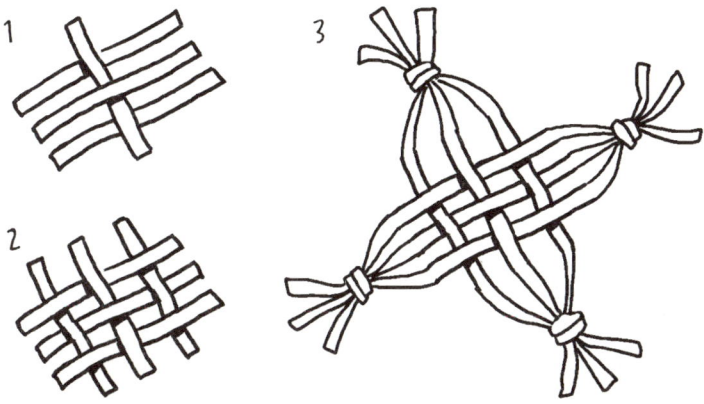

Flowers

To make spring daffodils, you will need:
  yellow paper patty pans
  cardboard and scissors
  glue
  straws or twigs
  stapler.

Draw around a patty pan on the cardboard. Now draw large petals and cut it all out. Staple the straw or twig (or a strip of cardboard) to the back of the flower for a stem. Glue the patty pan to the front. You could colour or paint the petals. Make a little bunch to put in a jar, or add leaves and glue them to a picture.

Hair-cutting dolls

Many kids are desperate to cut hair — their own, their priceless porcelain doll's, or yours. These little hair-cutting dolls are specifically designed to satisfy that urge!

You will need:
  cardboard rolls
  wool and scissors
  sticky tape
  (optional — material,
  glue and felt pens).

Cut lengths of wool, about 25 cm long. While the child holds the cardboard roll, you stretch the wool over the top of the roll so the 'hair' falls evenly down both sides. Now the child holds the hair on tightly while you wrap sticky tape right around the doll's head, $\frac{1}{2}$–1 cm from the top. You could be classy and cut a wee fringe.

Now if you like you can glue on strips of material for clothes, draw faces and arms, or just launch straight into your hairdressing apprenticeship!

Hole punch pottering

You will need:
- a hole punch
- paper and cardboard
- a needle and wool
- a screw-top jar and water.

There are several things you can do with the hole punch.

○ Fold a piece of paper in half twice (that is, in quarters). Punch around the outside. Now open it to see the pattern. Use it as a placemat or coaster.

○ Punch waxed paper. Open the hole punch into a jar of water and tip the little circles in. Screw the lid on and shake the jar for a 'snow' picture.

○ Make up a story about a worm eating a book. Staple your holey pages together and write the words around the holes.

○ Punch holes around the edge of a piece of cardboard. This could have already been cut in the shape of a fish, animal, star, Christmas tree and so on. Now sew wool in and out of the holes with a big needle. Tie it off when you get back to the start.

Invisible pictures

You will need:
- a white candle
- paper
- food colouring, dye or paint.

Draw a picture on the paper with the bottom end of the candle. Of course you can't see anything. To make the picture appear, paint the whole page with watered-down food colouring, dye or paint.

Islands

To make a model of an island you will need:
- an oven tray, or large square of thick cardboard, wood or polystyrene
- paint
- sand
- a swede or parsnip
- leafy twigs.

Paint the sea blue around the edge of the board. Then pile up sand in the middle, in an island shape. Pat it down firmly. Use blue paint to add rivers, which trickle down from the top, and white paint for roads, round the shoreline. Paint these on top of the sand.

Cut the swede or parsnip into tiny squares for houses, shops and churches, and larger shapes for schools and hospitals. Poke the twigs into the sand for trees growing on the island. You could also use the hole punch to cut out orange and white fruit, and glue these to your orange and coconut trees.

Literacy

These are games and activities to encourage literacy. You will need:
- books
- magnetic letters (choose these carefully if you are buying them. Lower case are better than capitals, and avoid the fancier letters, like *t a d*)
- paper
- cardboard
- pens
- scissors.

♥ Read to your child.

♥ Look at alphabet books and talk about the words that start with different letters. Talk about letter names and letter sounds.

- ♡ Play with magnetic letters. Make his name; let him copy it if he wants to. Let him make a 'word' with a whole jumble of letters. Try to read it back to him, pointing to where you are up to. This shows him that letters make sounds which can all be put together.

- ♡ Use your body to make letters. O is easy, but you need two people to make an M.

- ♡ Find words that rhyme with other words, words that start the same. Play 'I spy' and state what sound the word will start with.

- ♡ Make words by cutting letters out of newspapers, drawing them on card or forming letters with blocks, straws, food and so on.

- ♡ When she gives you a sentence to write down, use big clear words, then cut out the words. Jumble them, then remake the sentence.

- ♡ Let your child use the correction fluid. Ask him to white out every 'e' or 'a' from a line of large print. Some colouring books have captions in them and these are ideal.

- ♡ Set up a letter shop, as a game. You sell magnetic or cut-out letters to the customer, who comes in wanting to make a word. The customer will find it easier if there is an alphabet chart hanging in the shop.

- ♡ Let him see you reading! Be a role model!

Paint (see also 'Stamps')

Paper gets expensive when children paint a lot. Pull a page from a colouring book and let her paint that. Open out a plastic bag and paint onto the plastic. When it's dry you could stick it to the window for a good effect.

Try painting on different textures — old wallpaper, brown paper, wood, pinecones or a whole sheet of newspaper.

Mix paint with glue to get a gooey effect.

Paper plates

You will need:
- paper plates
- paint and glue
- elastic or wool
- a split pin and cardboard
- an old calendar
- staples and a little rice or some split peas and so on.

♡ Decorate paper plates for a party by painting them with non-toxic paints.

♡ Make party hats. Paint them, then attach wool to each side for tying under the chin, or tie a piece of elastic through holes at the two sides.

♡ Make a clock by cutting out numbers from a calendar and gluing them onto the paper plate. Cut out cardboard hands and attach these with a split pin through the hands then through the clock face.

♡ Make a tambourine. Place a handful of rice, split peas, dry beans or pebbles on one plate. Staple another plate on the top.

Plants

You will need:
- celery, food colouring
- potato, cotton wool, and some sort of seed, for example barley, wheat, mustard, lawn seed
- carrots
- pineapple
- onion, cardboard and a glass.

♡ Put a stick of celery in a glass of water that has a teaspoon of red food colouring in it. A day later, cut it in half and see how it has 'drunk' the coloured water. Explain how plants stay alive by sucking up moisture and nutrients.

- ♥ Potato man. Cut the bottom off a potato so it sits flat in a saucer with a little water in it. Scoop out the top so there is a little hollow, and place cotton wool in it. Sprinkle seed in the cotton wool, keep it watered and watch his 'hair' grow. You could add eyes and nose, with toothpicks and carrot rings.

- ♥ When you are cutting carrots for tea, place the green tops with a little of the orange piece in a saucer of water. Watch the green tops grow again.

- ♥ Try growing the leafy end plus 3 cm of the top of a pineapple. Let it dry out for ten days, then plant it in potting mix. Watch the interesting leaves grow.

- ♥ Onion flowers. Cut a circle of cardboard, and cut out the middle so the onion will sit in the cardboard. Place the circle of card over a glass full of water, so the root end of the onion sits in the water. Watch leaves and perhaps even a flower developing.

Polystyrene

Use the packaging from appliances to create castles and machines. Break the pieces up, and join them with toothpicks. You could paint your creation.

PVA prints

You will need:
    cardboard
    PVA glue
    paint and paper
    crayons and a small bottle.

Draw a picture on a piece of cardboard. Squirt PVA onto the pattern, leaving thick tracks. A day later you will have a lumpy, see-through pattern.

Experiment with different ways of printmaking. You could put paint on the lumpy pattern then turn it upside down onto a piece of paper. Rub the cardboard to make the pattern come through onto the page.

Or you could put the paper on top of the lumpy pattern, and rub crayon gently over the top. Try mixing colours. Or roll a small bottle in paint, and roll this over the paper.

Shaving cream

This is a rather expensive activity, but one day you'll be at your wits' end with a fractious child and it'll be worth it.

Squirt a bit of shaving cream or mousse onto the table and let him draw in it, write letters, make mountains. You could sprinkle in some powder paint for colour.

Stamps

You will need:
- paint
- a paper towel and a plate
- potatoes, fruit and a knife
- a polystyrene meat container
- a paintbrush.

Make a stamp pad by folding a paper towel in four, placing it on a plate, then pouring two teaspoons of paint into it. Now make stamps:

- ♡ Leaves. Press them gently into the stamp pad, then press onto a piece of paper.

- ♡ Cut a potato in half. Cut a shape into the cut side. Try a diamond or triangle to start with. Later on you might attempt to make letters, a tree or St Paul's Cathedral.

- ♡ Cut a fruit in half. The inside of an apple, orange, pear and so on makes an interesting shape.

CRAFTY IDEAS FOR PRESCHOOLERS

♡ Lie a polystyrene meat container upside down. Dig a pattern into it with the wrong end of a paintbrush, a spoon and so on. Now brush paint over the whole thing, then turn it over onto a piece of paper. Rub the inside bottom to make the pattern come out on your piece of paper.

♡ Other things which give a good effect with paint might include a piece of sponge, a piece of string dragged through paint then dragged over the page (try putting another piece of paper over the top), feathers and pumice.

Straw pictures

You will need:
>straw, for example pea straw, pampas foliage and so on
>scissors, glue and cardboard.

Cut the straw into thin strips. Glue these onto cardboard in the shape of a picture. A manger scene is a good place to start, and could be used as a Christmas card. Or make houses, mountains and letters of the alphabet.

Walnut shells

You will need:
>walnut shells
>playdough, toothpick and paper
>cotton wool.

♡ Use half an empty walnut shell to make a boat. Put a little playdough in, a toothpick for a mast, and a tiny paper sail.

♡ Make a bassinet by lying a little cotton wool in half an empty shell. Make a playdough baby if you don't have a tiny plastic one.

Party games for preschoolers

Dress-up bag

Pass around a large bag, which is not see-through and is full of dress-up clothes. When the music stops, the child holding the bag must shut his eyes, stick his hand in, and put on whatever he finds.

What's the time, Mr Wolf?

In case your memory is fuzzy, it goes like this: children line up along a wall. Mr Wolf stands one metre ahead, facing away from the others. As the children call, 'What's the time, Mr Wolf?' they, and he, walk slowly away from the wall. Mr Wolf calls, 'Two o'clock', 'Four o'clock' and so on. When he calls 'Dinnertime!', he turns around for the first time. The children all run back to the wall where they are safe. If he catches one before she reaches the wall, she becomes the new Mrs (or Ms) Wolf.

Shapes

Use a large piece of plastic or an old sheet, about two metres square, and draw coloured shapes on it like a green triangle, an orange circle, a blue square. Make a die by drawing the same coloured shapes onto six sides of a square of wood, or make a cardboard die out of a shape like that shown on the next page, sticky-taped together.

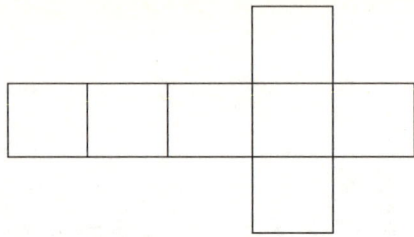

Each child takes a turn to throw the die. He must place one foot on whatever shape he throws. On his next turn he places a hand, then another foot and so on. The winner is the last one to fall over.

Treasure hunt

Draw pictures of the places you want the children to look, in order to find the clues. Your clues might look something like this.

When you are placing the clues, work backwards from the treasure; it is less confusing.

Newspaper war

If you don't mind clearing up a big mess, this is great for allowing kids to let off steam. Divide them into two teams. Lie a piece of string down the centre of the room to mark halfway. Give each team a pile of newspapers, and five minutes to scrunch it into balls. On 'Go', everyone throws their balls of newspaper onto the other team's side. If they have any energy left at the end, play it again, and again, and again …

Some fun ideas for school-aged children

Baking

1. Try making **ice blocks**. Pour juice into yoghurt pottles. Attach a stick by making a small hole in the middle of the tinfoil yoghurt lid, put the lid on and slide the stick down to the bottom of the pottle. Freeze it.

2. **Never Fail Chocolate Cake**
    - 75 g melted butter
    - 100 g flour
    - 150 g sugar
    - 2 Tbsp cocoa
    - 2 Tbsp milk
    - 3 eggs
    - 2 tsp baking powder

    Mix all the ingredients, except the baking powder, for 4 minutes. Stir in the baking powder. Pour into a cake tin that has been greased and bake at 180°C for about 20 minutes. Ice when cold.

3. **Double Chocolate Muffins** (makes 12)
    - 1¾ cups flour
    - 1 tsp baking soda
    - 1 cup sugar

SOME FUN IDEAS FOR SCHOOL-AGED CHILDREN

    ¼ cup cocoa
    100 g butter
    1 egg
    1 cup yoghurt (or 1 cup milk and 1 tsp lemon juice)
    ½ cup milk
    ½ tsp vanilla
    ¼–½ cup of chocolate chips

Sift the dry ingredients into one bowl. In another bowl, melt the butter and add the rest of the ingredients. Mix these until they are smooth. Pour this into the dry ingredients, and stir it until it is only just combined. Don't mix it any more!

Spray with oil or grease muffin pans. Fill with mixture. Sprinkle the chocolate chips on top and bake at 200°C for 10–12 minutes.

Leave for 3 minutes, then tip them out onto a rack.

4 Fudge

    2 cups sugar
    ½ cup milk
    1 Tbsp cocoa
    25 g butter
    ½ tsp vanilla

Heat the first four ingredients gradually, until the butter is melted. Then boil it for 4 minutes, stirring all the time. Add the vanilla. Beat it until it is starting to set, then pour it into a greased dish.

5 Pancakes (feeds 6 people)

    2½ cups flour
    2½ tsp baking powder
    ½ cup sugar
    pinch of salt
    2 eggs
    1–2 Tbsp melted butter
    2¼ cups milk

SOME FUN IDEAS FOR SCHOOL-AGED CHILDREN

Sift the dry ingredients into a bowl. Put the other ingredients into another bowl. Make a well in the dry mixture, pour in the wet ingredients and mix from the centre out.

Lightly grease a heavy frypan that is heated to about a quarter of its full heat of the element. Pour in about 3 tablespoons of mixture. Flip it when bubbles form on the top.

Stack them on a plate as they become ready, with a small piece of lunch paper between each one. Keep them warm.

Meanwhile make the caramel sauce:

    ¾ cup water
    3 heaped Tbsp brown sugar
    1 large Tbsp golden syrup

Boil these in a pot. Then thicken with 3 heaped teaspoons of cornflour and 2 tablespoons water mixed in a cup.

Pour the sauce over two or three pancakes on a plate. Whipped cream is nice and so is bacon. Yum!

6 Self-Saucing Microwave Pudding

    1 cup self-raising flour
    1 Tbsp cocoa
    ⅓ cup sugar
    ½ cup milk
    1 tsp vanilla
    30 g butter
    ¾ cup brown sugar
    ¾ cup water
    another 2 Tbsp cocoa

Sift flour and 1 tablespoon cocoa into a bowl. Add sugar, milk and vanilla, and mix well. Melt butter and add. Press the mixture into a large microwave bowl.

Mix the last three ingredients and pour it over the pudding, then cook on high for 4 to 6 minutes.

Boats

1. Remember pooh sticks? Everyone chooses a stick and throws it off one side of a bridge into a river. Looking carefully for traffic, cross the bridge and see whose stick arrives first. By the way — start on the upstream side!

2. Decorate a bottle. Have a competition to see whose 'boat' goes the fastest down a stream. You could use this as a party idea — everyone brings a boat and you judge them on a) appearance, b) sea worthiness, and c) speed.

3. Fold over a leaf and poke the stem into the leaf halfway down.

4. Make a raft out of black flax flower stems that are tied together with string. Stick a barbecue skewer into it for a mast and attach a paper sail.

Christmas decorations

▮ **Christmas trees**

You will need:
 paper
 sticky tape
 scissors.

Lie about four sheets of paper on top of each other (glossy junk mail works well). Roll them up from one end, not too tight, but so you could put your finger easily down inside. Sticky tape it shut. Now cut down the roll to about halfway. Do this three more times, so the roll is cut in quarters, to halfway. Now grab the inside strands and pull them up, then pull the branches down gently.

 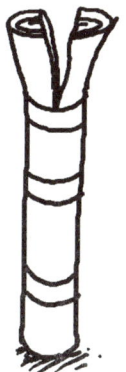 

▮ **Muriel's lanterns**

You will need:
 paper
 scissors.

Make a square of fairly thick paper (like photocopy paper) by folding it diagonally, drawing a line where the fold comes to, and cutting off the single rectangle. Throw that away.

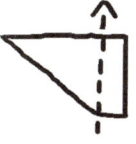

Take the triangle piece and fold it again diagonally, then again.

Hold the tip and with scissors cut a strip about 5 mm thick from the wide end. Start at the side where there are three folds and head towards the end with one fold. Stop 1 cm before the end, so it is not cut right through.

Now turn it over in your hand, and cut another strip, this time from the one-fold side to the three-fold side.

Repeat these two cuts right up the triangle.

Now lie it down on the table and open out the last diagonal fold, then the next, then the last one until you have a square.

Turn the square over so there is a little peak standing up. Put your hand up inside this peak and with your other hand, gently pull the bottom sides down.

When you have made it successfully, try again, but cut the strips even thinner.

3. **Nativity scene**

> *You will need:*
>> a 1.5 litre plastic soft drink bottle
>> playdough
>> old Christmas cards.

Cut an oval shape from the front of the bottle, about 14 cm high, 13 cm wide, and 4 cm from the bottom. Fill the bottom with playdough.

SOME FUN IDEAS FOR SCHOOL-AGED CHILDREN

Using old Christmas cards, cut out Mary, Joseph, Baby Jesus, lambs and so on, and push these into the playdough so they stand up. Suspend a star from the top of the bottle.

4 Pine cone table centre
You will need:
- a pine cone
- PVA glue
- glitter
- twigs.

Splash PVA glue onto a pine cone. Sprinkle glitter over it, or empty the hole punch over it. When it's dry, stick twigs of macrocarpa, holly and so on in the pine cone.

5 Wrapping paper
You will need:
- paper
- paint
- potato
- knife
- paper towel.

Make a potato stamp (see 'Stamps' on page 122). Use this to make a repeated pattern on a large piece of paper.

Dough baskets

You will need:
- 4 cups flour
- 1½ cups salt
- 1½ cups water
- egg yolk
- an oven tray and an ovenproof bowl

Make a dough from the flour, salt and water.

SOME FUN IDEAS FOR SCHOOL-AGED CHILDREN

Turn the ovenproof bowl upside down and grease the underside.

Make sausages from the dough and lie about five of these all one way, across the bowl, with about 2 cm spare over the edges.

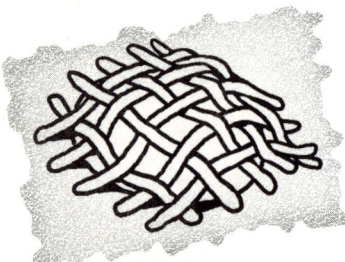

Now roll out five more, lie these across the bowl the other way, lifting up every second sausage you come to, so you 'weave' the sausages.

Now twist two very long sausages together and lie this around the top of the bowl (which at the moment is at the bottom), tucking the ends of the weaving in as you go.

Brush on a glaze of an egg yolk mixed with 2 tablespoons of water.

Put the whole thing onto an oven tray, and cook very slowly at 90°C for nine hours.

When cold, varnish and sprinkle sesame or celery seeds around the top while the varnish is wet.

SOME FUN IDEAS FOR SCHOOL-AGED CHILDREN

Easter ideas

1. Decorate a hard-boiled egg with felt pens or paint.

2. Try this game which European children play on Easter Monday.

   Children decorate and name their egg, then everyone rolls their egg down a slope, possibly with the assistance of wooden spoons. The last one to crack is the winner.

3. Blow an egg

   Use a sharp needle to poke a small hole at both ends of a raw egg. Gently blow out the contents through the larger hole, then carefully wash out the empty shell, sit in an eggcup and paint.

   Plan to have scrambled eggs today. It could take several attempts!

4. Flannelgraph Easter story

   Draw pictures of Jesus, the women who visited the tomb, the angel, the rock. Cut them out and stick them onto pieces of flannelette sheet. Paint a background scene, including a cave for the tomb, on a large piece of the sheet. Stick the figures on as you tell the story.

Mr Squidgy

You will need:
- a balloon
- clay
- plastic eyes
- flexible contact adhesive glue (Selley's Quik Grip is good)
- a tiny piece of sheepskin
- cotton
- scissors.

Cut the neck from the balloon, and fill it with about half a cup of clay. Tie the top with cotton. Glue a small square of sheepskin over the tied top, for hair, or make a pompom (see below).

Glue on little eyes, which can be bought for a few cents at a craft shop, and a nose made from a button, piece of sheepskin or curl of wool.

When the glue is dry make facial expressions by pushing in with your thumbs. Be careful not to pop the balloon with sharp nails.

A simplified Mr Squidgy has playdough or flour inside the balloon. It is quite good, although the expressions don't stay as sharp. Draw on eyes and nose with felt pen.

Pine cone families

You will need:
   tiny pine cones, PVA, flat piece of driftwood, eyes, buttons, wool.

Glue tiny pine cones onto the driftwood. Glue on eyes, or use buttons and wool for the eyes and mouth.

Plaiting

You will need:
   wool.

Make colourful bracelets for wrists or ankles by plaiting wool. Cut three lengths of wool, about 50 cm long. Tie them together at one end and get someone to hold it for you. Holding the three ends firmly, pass the outside strands alternately over the top of the middle one. Tie at the end.

Pompoms

You will need:
   cardboard or plastic
   wool
   scissors.

Make two circles of plastic (ice cream lids are ideal) or cardboard. Start with very small ones, about 4–5 cm diameter. Use a craft knife to cut a circle from the centre of them (about 2 cm diameter) (1).

SOME FUN IDEAS FOR SCHOOL-AGED CHILDREN

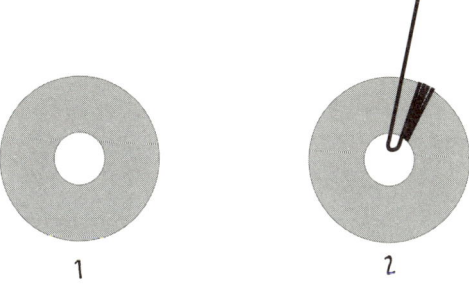

1 2

Cut a metre of wool. Wind it round and round the face of the circle, by passing the wool through the centre and over the outside (2), until the whole of the plastic is covered. Change the colour of wool if desired, and wind another layer over the circle.

Now snip around the outside edge of the wool by forcing the scissors between the two circles of plastic.

When it is cut right around, tie a piece of wool tightly between the two circles, then slip them off. If you have made it a very full pompom, cut the circles off.

Try making bigger and bigger pompoms.

Tie-dyeing

Buy a tin of dye from a pharmacy.

Tie knots in a white T-shirt, or scrunch up bunches of the fabric and tie them tightly with string. You could tie-dye night shirts, hankies, wall hangings, sarongs or shirts.

Follow the directions on the dye packet.

Stilts

You will need to buy:

    4 m plane and gauge wood (sanded), about 45 mm x 35 mm
    another piece of wood, about 140 mm long, 35 mm x 80 mm
    a sheet of sandpaper, medium grade
    strong hardware glue, with the strength of nails.

SOME FUN IDEAS FOR SCHOOL-AGED CHILDREN

Cut the long piece of wood in half, so you have two stilts, each about 2 m long. Hold the wood in a vice to saw.

Cut the smaller piece into two foot-pieces, each 70 mm long.

Lie each stilt on the ground. Place the foot-piece on the narrow (35 mm) edge of the stilt, about 25 cm from the ground. Mark the stilt with a pencil to show where the foot-piece goes.

Take the foot-piece off. Follow the directions on the glue packet to attach the foot-piece to the stilt, on your pencil mark.

When the glue is dry, rub all the wood with sandpaper until it is smooth all over.

To walk on stilts: stand with the bottoms of the stilts on the ground in front of you, and the top ends behind your shoulders. Have someone hold them from behind, or lean against a wall to get started. Your arms will be straight, holding right around each stilt with your thumbs facing forward. Lift each stilt as you walk. Don't give up! You'll get it after a few more tries!

Further reading

At the Cutting Edge. By Tom Nicholson. NZ Council for Educational Research: 1994. Research that shows what parents of good readers did to help.

Bedwetting. By Glen Stenhouse and Michael Watt. Government Printing Office. Some good ideas in an intensive programme to help over-sixes.

Catch Them When They're Good: A Parents' Guide to Survival. By David Stewart. Dunmore Press.

Children's Language Development. By Anne McDonell. Government Printing Office.

Dare to Discipline. By Dr James Dobson. Kingsway Publication. Very good and practical about discipline.

Everybody Hurts Sometimes: a book about grief for children and teenagers. By Lois Tonkin. Port Hills Press. Available from Lois Tonkin, 343 Port Hills Road, Christchurch.

The Five Love Languages of Children. By Gary Chapman and Ross Campbell. Scripture Press.

Good Behaviour. By Fred Seymour, Leslie Centre. GP Publications. A step-by-step guide to changing children's behaviour.

How to Really Love Your Child. By Dr Ross Campbell. Scripture Press. How to make them experience the love you feel.

Nobody Likes Me: Helping Your Child Make Friends. By Elaine K. McEwan. Harold Shaw Publishers.

Pyjamas Don't Matter. By Trish Gribben. Heinemann. Very sound, practical advice about babies and toddlers.

FURTHER READING

The Secret of Happy Children. By Steve Biddulph. Bay Books. Very readable.

The Sixty-Minute Father. By Rob Parsons. Hodder and Stoughton. Inspiring. A dad speaks about how he nearly missed out on his kids' lives.

The Sleep Book. By Kathy MacDonald, Leslie Centre. Reed. Excellent. A small but practical book. It works!

A Volcano in My Tummy. By Éliane Whitehouse and Warwick Pudney. Peace Foundation. A good resource for helping children deal with anger.

Who Switched the Price Tags? By Tony Campolo. Word USA. A good look at what's really important. Some interesting insights into the place of ritual in children's lives.